W9-BPR-299

DATE DUE

MUIRHEAD LIBRARY OF PHILOSOPHY

An admirable statement of the aims of the Library of Philosophy was provided by the first editor, the late Professor J. H. Muirhead, in his description of the original programme printed in Erdmann's *History of Philosophy* under the date 1890. This was slightly modified in subsequent volumes to take the form of the following statement:

'The Muirhead Library of Philosophy was designed as a contribution to the History of Modern Philosophy under the heads: first of Different Schools of Thought—Sensationalist, Realist, Idealist, Intuitivist; secondly of different Subjects—Psychology, Ethics, Aesthetics, Political Philosophy, Theology. While much had been done in England in tracing the course of evolution in nature, history, economics, morals and religion, little had been done in tracing the development of thought on these subjects. Yet the "evolution of opinion is part of the whole evolution".

'By the cooperation of different writers in carrying out this plan it was hoped that a thoroughness and completeness of treatment, otherwise unattainable, might be secured. It was believed also that from writers mainly British and American fuller consideration of English Philosophy than it had hitherto received might be looked for. In the earlier series of books containing, among others, Bosanquet's *History of Aesthetics*, Pfleiderer's *Rational Theology since Kant*, Albee's *History of English Utilitarianism*, Bonar's *Philosophy and Political Economy*, Brett's *History of Psychology*, Ritchie's *Natural Rights*, these objects were to a large extent effected.

'In the meantime original work of a high order was being produced both in England and America by such writers as Bradley, Stout, Bertrand Russell, Baldwin, Urban, Montague, and others, and a new interest in foreign works, German, French and Italian, which had either become classical or were attracting public attention, had developed. The scope of the Library thus became extended into something more international, and it is entering on the fifth decade of its existence in the hope that it may contribute to that mutual understanding between countries which is so pressing a need of the present time.'

The need which Professor Muirhead stressed is no less pressing today, and few will deny that philosophy has much to do with enabling us to meet it, although no one, least of all Muirhead himself, would regard that as the sole, or even the main, object of philosophy. As Professor Muirhead continues to lend the distinction of his name to the Library of Philosophy it seemed not inappropriate to allow him to recall us to these aims in his own words. The emphasis on the history of thought also seemed to me very timely : and the number of important works promised for the Library in the very near future augur well for the continued fulfilment, in this and other ways, of the expectations of the original editor.

H. D. LEWIS

MUIRHEAD LIBRARY OF PHILOSOPHY

General Editor: H. D. Lewis

Professor of History and Philosophy of Religion at the University of London

The Absolute and the Atonement by DOM ILLTYD TRETHOWAN

Absolute Value by DOM ILLYD TRETHOWAN

The Analysis of Mind by BERTRAND RUSSELL

Ascent to the Absolute by J. N. FINDLAY

Belief by H. H. PRICE

Broad's Critical Essays in Moral Philosophy edited by DAVID CHENEY

Clarity is Not Enough by H. D. LEWIS

Coleridge as Philosopher by J. H. MUIRHEAD

The Commonplace Book of G. E. Moore edited by C. LEWY

The Concept of Meaning by THOMAS E. HILL

Contemporary American Philosophy edited by G. P. ADAMS and W. P. MONTAGUE

Contemporary British Philosophy first and second series edited by J. H. MUIRHEAD 2nd edition

Contemporary British Philosophy third series edited by H. D. LEWIS

Contemporary Indian Philosophy edited by RADHAKRISHNAN and J. H. MUIRHEAD 2nd edition

Contemporary Philosophy in Australia edited by ROBERT BROWN and C. D. ROLLINS

The Development of Bertrand Russell's Philosophy by RONALD JAGER

The Dilemma of Narcissus by LOUIS LAVELLE

The Discipline of the Cave by J. N. FINDLAY

Enigmas of Agency by IRVING THALBURG

Essays in Analysis by ALICE AMBROSE

Ethical Knowledge by J. J. KUPPERMAN

Ethics by NICOLAI HARTMANN translated by STANTON COIT 3 vols

Ethics and Christianity by KEITH WARD

Experimental Realism by A. H. JOHNSON

The Foundation of Metaphysics in Science by ERROL E. HARRIS

Freedom and History by H. D. LEWIS

Reason and Goodness by BRAND BLANSHARD
Reason and Scepticism by MICHAEL A. SLOTE
The Science of Logic by G. W. F. HEGEL
Some Main Problems of Philosophy by G. E. MOORE
The Subject of Consciousness by C. O. EVANS
Time and Free Will by HENRI BERGSON translated by F. G. POGSON
Value and Reality by A. C. EWING
Varieties of Belief by PAUL HELM

MUIRHEAD LIBRARY OF PHILOSOPHY

EDITED BY H. D. LEWIS

PHILOSOPHY
AND
PSYCHICAL
RESEARCH

PHILOSOPHY
AND
PSYCHICAL
RESEARCH

Edited by

SHIVESH C. THAKUR
MA, PhD
Professor of Philosophy, University of Surrey

LONDON GEORGE ALLEN & UNWIN LTD
NEW YORK HUMANITIES PRESS INC

First published in 1976

© George Allen & Unwin 1976

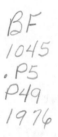

Library of Congress Cataloging in Publication Data
Main entry under title:

Philosophy and psychical research.

(Muirhead library of phiolsophy)
Includes index.
1. Parapsychology and philosophy — Addresses, essays, lectures. 2. Religion and parapsychology — Addresses, essays, lectures. I. Thakur, Shivesh Chandra. II. Series; Library of phiolsophy.
BF1045.P5P49 1976   133.8'01   75-45186   ISBN 0-391-00538-3

Printed in The United States of America

PREFACE

There are those—not necessarily psychical researchers themselves
—who believe that psychical research is already an established,
though young, scientific discipline. Many are sceptical. Whichever opinion is correct, there is little doubt that the claims of
psychical research seem, *prima facie,* to have implications for
certain important philosophical issues and concepts. Understandably, philosophers—of widely differing persuasions—have
been interested in psychical research. But the full extent of this
interest has not generally been known either to professional philosophers or to psychical researchers. This volume is intended,
partly at least, to set the record straight.

A number of well-known philosophers were invited to write on
whichever philosophical issue relating to psychical research interested them most. This volume is a collection of essays that
were received in response. There are many philosophers who
would have been happy to write but were unable to do so—mostly
due to other commitments. It is hoped that the essays that appear
here will serve to show not only the extent of interest in psychical
research on the part of professional philosophers but also the
reasons for such interest. If the volume succeeds in creating some
new interest in the subject, it will have achieved all its aims.

The first essay is by a psychologist, and was intended—partly
at least—to serve as an introduction, which, it was felt, might
help readers not already familiar with the field of psychical research. Consequently, this essay appears first. The rest of them
appear under the names of their authors, in alphabetical order.

I am grateful to all the contributors to the volume for their
positive response. My special thanks are due to Professor H. D.
Lewis for his constant help and encouragement; to Dr D. M. A.
Leggett, Vice-Chancellor, University of Surrey, whose abiding
passion for psychical research was instrumental in my acquiring
a major interest in the subject; to George Allen & Unwin for
agreeing to publish the volume; to my secretary, Mrs L. M. Ball,

for retyping some of the material and duplicating all of it; and to my wife, Philippa, for helping with the correction of the proofs.

SHIVESH THAKUR
University of Surrey
Guildford

CONTENTS

I

ESP AND ATTEMPTS TO
EXPLAIN IT

by

ALAN GAULD

' . . . the Devil hath great power in ruling that which they
call *Chance*.'
    Richard Baxter, *Certainty of the World of Spirits* (1691)

It will be convenient to begin with some definitions offered by
Mundle (1967). ESP, or extrasensory perception, is 'the acquisition of information without the use of any human sense organs'.
The main subspecies of ESP are *telepathy*, in which 'the information originates from the mind of another person', *clairvoyance*, in
which 'the information originates from physical objects', and *precognition*, in which 'the information is about *and originates from*
future events'. We may also note the terms *retrocognition*—ESP
in which the information is about and originates from past
events, and *psychokinesis* (PK)—the direct influence of mental
events on physical events external to the agent's body. These
definitions are, as Mundle points out, not altogether satisfactory;
but for immediate purposes they will suffice.

The evidence for ESP may be divided into the anecdotal and
the experimental (a recent review is Thouless, 1972). We have on
the one hand a large number of apparently authentic reports of
the unsought, 'spontaneous' occurrence of ESP in the shape of
premonitions, hunches, telepathic dreams, overpowering emotional
upsurges, irresistible impulses to action, persistent vivid images,
and actual hallucinations of persons, voices or distant scenes; and

on the other hand increasingly numerous attempts to demonstrate comparable, though usually much less exciting, phenomena by properly designed laboratory experiments. Somewhere between anecdote and experiment come investigations of ESP apparently exhibited in such phenomena as automatic writing, automatic speaking and crystal visions.

The earliest large-scale attempts to collect and classify firsthand reports of spontaneously occurring ESP were those made towards the end of the last century by certain leading members of the British Society for Psychical Research (the SPR). In 1886, four years after the SPR was founded, it published the monumental two-volumed *Phantasms of the Living* by Edmund Gurney, F. W. H. Myers and F. Podmore. Gurney, the principal author, was a man of exceptional abilities, and his classification of cases and discussion of the psychology of testimony in regard to unusual events have remained classics in the field. These early writers would probably have felt that the anecdotal evidence alone was sufficient to establish that ESP occurs. This is an arguable point of view. Modern parapsychologists, however, have tended to follow modern psychologists in their (perhaps excessive) respect for laboratory experiments, and many of them would regard collections of spontaneous cases as of value chiefly in suggesting hypotheses which can be subjected to more stringent investigation in the laboratory (e.g. Thouless, 1972, p. 16).

For many years laboratory experimentation on ESP was popularly equated with the card-guessing techniques pioneered by Professor J. B. Rhine of Duke University in the early 1930s, and brought to their highest pitch of statistical success by Dr S. G. Soal in the early 1940s. Work in this tradition is still carried out, but of late it has been partly overshadowed by experiments utilising electronic machinery for the presentation and randomisation of target sequences and for the recording of subjects' guesses. Extremely influential here have been some experiments on precognition by Schmidt (1969). Schmidt used small numbers of subjects whom there was some antecedent reason for regarding as possibly 'gifted'. The targets were four electric lamps of different colours. The subjects' task was to indicate, by pressing the appropriate button, which lamp they thought would light next. Which lamp in fact lit was determined by the closure of an electronic switch which designated each lamp in turn a quarter of a million times every second. Between the pressing of the button and the closure of the switch there was a delay of about one tenth of a second. The precise length of this delay was determined by the decay of a piece of radio-active strontium 90, a process which, as far as is known, is quite random. The output sequences of this machine were extensively tested for 'randomness'. In one series of experiments three subjects made between them 63,066 guesses. 'Hits' exceeded chance expectation by just over 690 (odds greater than 500 million to 1). In another series of 20,000 guesses, four subjects were asked to pick a lamp which would *not* light. Their success was so great that the odds against its being due to chance exceeded 10 thousand million to 1.

Schmidt and others have subsequently carried out similar experiments. Using eleven subjects who did not claim to be gifted, and Schmidt's machine, Haraldson (1970) obtained odds of 2,000 to 1 against chance. Targ and Hunt (1971) with a machine of their own design which incorporated various devices for encouraging successful subjects, claimed that three out of twenty subjects tested for clairvoyance showed significant 'learning' over several hundred to several thousand guesses. One of the three, a girl of 10, scored so highly in her later trials that her overall mean score per run for 64 runs of 24 guesses was 8·6 where 6 was expected (odds against chance greater than 10^{15} to 1). Kelly and Kanthamami (1972) utilised Schmidt's machine in the course of testing a somewhat volatile subject who claimed to have had remarkable 'spontaneous' ESP experiences. In a run of 508 trials he made 180 hits (odds against chance in excess of 10 million to 1). In an informal series of 329 trials he played the machine with the target lamps off (misses produced a single click, hits a double click). His score of 163 exceeded chance by greatly over 10 thousand million to 1. A punched tape was then connected to the machine to record guesses and hits trial by trial. This disturbed the subject, whose scores (with lamps restored) declined markedly. However, he determined to beat the machine, and over the whole series of 5,377 trials he made 1,542 hits (odds against chance greater than a thousand million to 1). Bierman and Camastra (1973) have devised an automated procedure for classroom ESP testing. They tested 1,402 pupils from twelve schools, and obtained a mean score of 16·034 per run where chance expectation was 15 (odds against chance in excess of 10^{30} to 1).

Automation would seem to have been carried to its limit in certain ESP experiments with animals. The first of these experiments was published pseudonymously by two French biologists (Duval and Montredon, 1968). They used a specially designed cage divided into two compartments by a low hurdle. The floor of the cage was an electric grid through which a mild shock could be delivered to the animal inside. Mice were placed in the cage, which was alone in the experimental room, one at a time. Before each trial the cage was illuminated and the position of the mouse was recorded by means of a system of photoelectric cells. If the mouse was in that half of the cage selected by a multivibrator in another room, it received a shock. The mouse's task was thus on each trial to avoid that half of the cage which was about to be shocked. Four mice were given twenty-five runs of from 100 to 140 trials, each run being electronically controlled. On the majority of trials the animals showed 'static' or 'mechanical' behaviour—they remained in the side of the cage which had proved safe on the previous trial, and, if they received a shock, jumped into the other half of the cage. Occasionally they showed what the experimenters called 'random' behaviour—they moved out of the previously safe side. Out of the 612 trials on which 'random' behaviour took place, the mice avoided the shock 359 times (odds against chance greater than 1,000 to 1). These findings have supposedly been confirmed in the United States and in Holland by about a dozen published experiments using small rodents as subjects, but a certain doubt now hangs over a number of these.

For the purposes of this paper I shall assume that the evidence for ESP is satisfactory. The brief account of it given above is more an attempt to characterise the present state of play than to soften the unconvinced. Indeed, there are those among the unconvinced who would take a good deal of softening. This may in part be because some of those who believe in ESP have suggested that its occurence forces various philosophical conclusions upon us. For example Price (1949, p. 109) has said, 'There is no room for telepathy in a Materialistic universe'. I shall shortly consider certain attempts to show that ESP can only be explained or understood in ways which force upon us particular philosophical positions or frameworks of thought. But before doing so, I shall very briefly outline some of the empirical findings (or alleged findings) which might be thought likely to have relevance to the theoretical explanations of ESP. This can conveniently be done under three headings, as follows :

(a) An obvious preliminary question to ask is this : Is there any need to look for different or differing explanations of telepathy, clairvoyance and precognition? It might be the case, for example, that the findings which have hitherto been regarded as evidence for telepathy can be shown on further investigation to be instances of clairvoyance. Many early experimenters took it for granted that if an 'agent' in one room concentrated upon, say, a drawing, and a 'percipient' in the next room successfully reproduced that drawing, then mind had contacted mind directly. But of course if clairvoyance be a fact, the percipient might have obtained his information about the drawing clairvoyantly, in which case the agent's concentration would have been so much wasted effort. To decide between these possibilities it is only necessary to set up experiments in which the 'targets' remain in the mind of the agent until after the percipient has made his guess, and experiments in which the targets remain unknown to anyone until after the percipient has made his guesses. The first person to conduct such experiments systematically was J. B. Rhine, and significant results were obtained under both telepathic and clairvoyant conditions.

The problems become much more complex, however, if we admit, as we must, that the evidence for precognition is at least as strong as the evidence for telepathy and for clairvoyance. If precognition is a possibility, then successful subjects in 'telepathy' experiments may obtain their results by precognitive clairvoyance of the written record which the experimenter makes *after* the agent has guessed; and successful subjects in 'clairvoyance' experiments may obtain their results by precognitive telepathy with the mind of the experimenter as he inspects the target sequences after the experiment. To design 'pure' telepathy or 'pure' clairvoyance experiments is rather tricky, but such experiments have been designed and positive results claimed in them (see Mundle, op. cit., for a detailed review of the problem). Pure clairvoyance is in principle demonstrated if a subject can score above chance on a machine which presents targets in a random sequence, provided that the targets are not visible to or inferable by the experimenter or anyone else, and provided that the machine records only the number of hits, i.e. not the target or guess sequences. Pure telepathy is in principle demonstrated if, by means of a purely private code, the 'agent' can link targets held 'in the mind' to the digit sequences of a series of random numbers, provided that no public record is made detailing which of the percipient's guesses were correct and which not, and only the total number of correct guesses per run is actually set down.

On the face of it, therefore, we have evidence both for pure telepathy and for pure clairvoyance. The following two qualifications must, however, be made. Firstly, someone might suggest that all cases of ostensible telepathy can be written off as examples of the clairvoyant apprehension of another person's brain-state; this view would no doubt be supported by philosophical and physiological considerations. But it leaves open at least as many problems as it solves. Ordinary clairvoyance (if one may speak of it like that) tends to be of the macroscopic properties of commonplace physical objects; 'telepathic' clairvoyance (to coin a phrase) would have to be of the microscopic and possibly subatomic properties of brains, and would require the percipient to have an infinitely greater ability to interpret and understand such properties than any neurologist of this century (and probably the next few centuries too). Furthermore, it is, as we shall see, even harder to conceive of a physical explanation for clairvoyance than it is to imagine one for telepathy.

Secondly, it might be proposed that precognition itself can be understood in terms of telepathic or clairvoyant cognition of contemporary states of affairs from which the precognised event can be predicted. This would require percipients to possess, presumably unawares, powers of prediction vastly in excess of those of the most able mathematical physicists; and besides that, in the experiments of Schmidt (1969) mentioned above, one of the factors influencing the determination of the target was the decay of a piece of a radioactive substance, a process unpredictable in the requisite detail.

A final possibility which should be mentioned is that successful results in telepathy and precognition experiments may be due to PK on the part of the subjects. It has, for instance, been proposed that telepathy may be due to the agent's causing the firing of 'critically poised' neurons in the percipient's brain. But this seems once again to require that agents must possess unawares a vastly greater knowledge of brain function than any neurophysiologist, and in addition raises the question of how, other than by clairvoyance, the agent is able to locate the 'critically poised' neurons which, with a particular target and a particular percipient, it is appropriate for him to influence. In the case of the more striking 'spontaneous' precognitions, the idea that agents bring about the fulfilment of their 'precognitions' by psychokinesis must surely be dismissed as preposterous. It would involve us in saying that such events as the sinking of the *Titanic* were brought about by the monitory dreams of those who foresaw the disaster. In the case of certain small-scale laboratory experiments on 'precognition' the idea is not so preposterous—indeed there were some indications that one of Schmidt's successful subjects may have achieved his results in this way. Schmidt and Pantas (1972) investigated the possibility further in a highly ingenious experiment. Schmidt's original precognition machine was altered in such a way that by the flip of a switch it could, unknown to the subject, be changed into a machine on which they could only get results by PK. When the subject pressed a button to indicate a guess, and the randon number generator produced a 1, 2, 3, or 4, the 1, 2, 3, or 0 lamp position to the right was lit. Thus subjects could only score above chance by 'forcing' the machine to generate 4s. Fairly significant above chance scores were in fact obtained under both conditions.

The upshot of this involved discussion seems to be that, of the subspecies of ESP cited at the beginning, only retrocognition can perhaps be interpreted in terms of the others and thus eliminated. For if any supposed example of retrocognition is to be confirmed, the information which will verify it must exist *now*, and must accordingly be in principle accessible to telepathy or to clairvoyance. (Perhaps, however, a retrocognitive vision of such an object as Fermat's proof of his last theorem might turn out to be self-verifying.) Despite this obstinate refusal of the various sub-species of ESP to be eliminated, it is very commonly supposed that they are at root manifestations of the same underlying process. The reasons why this is maintained appear to be : that persons who seem to possess one of the kinds of ESP commonly also exhibit the others; that the ways in which the various sub-species of ESP spontaneously manifest themselves (in symbols, in phenomena which intrude on the normal course of conscious-ness, and so on) are pretty much the same, and so are the matters to which they relate; that conditions which favour or hinder one kind of ESP commonly also favour or hinder the others; and that in some spontaneous cases there are features suggestive of the con-joint working of telepathy and clairvoyance.

These considerations do not seem to me to go very far towards establishing the desired conclusion. For if it be true (and it is, as we shall shortly see, commonly alleged) that information acquired by ESP is usually, as it were, detained in and processed by some unconscious level of the personality before finding its way into consciousness, then the similarities in form of manifestation, and in the conditions favourable to manifestation, can readily be explained without supposing that the underlying process of ESP is in each instance the same. In fact, the ways in which ESP manifests itself show certain similarities to the ways in which sub-liminal perceptions of an ordinary kind, and also long-forgotten memories, may find expression (Beloff, 1972; cf. Dixon, 1971). And so if someone produces a theoretical explanation of ESP which, for instance, covers telepathy but not clairvoyance, we should not (as some have tended to do) on that account reject it. Rather we should be thankful for even a partial illumination of this obscure field.

(b) Many of the persons who have studied the evidence for ESP have been led to the same conclusion about the underlying process (or processes), namely that it affects in the first place some unconscious or subliminal level of the personality, and thence may burst into consciousness, or filter through to consciousness in some disguised form, or that it may indeed express itself inde-pendently of consciousness in the shape of some motor auto-matism or even psychokinetic phenomenon. The reasons why this conclusion has so often appeared compelling seem to be these. Firstly, many of the phenomena in which ESP is characteristically manifested are, as regards the subject's ordinary stream of consciousness, alien, intrusive and uncontrollable. One might instance automatic writing, veridical hallucinations, and 'true' dreams. And it is worth noting that the guesses of successful subjects in laboratory ESP experiments—their card calls, button presses etc.—tend to be automatic rather than to be based upon inner images or intuitions. Secondly, the phenomena in which ESP is characteristically manifested are often ones which are regarded for other reasons as expressing levels of intelligent functioning not ordinarily accessible to consciousness. Here again one might instance automatic writing and dreams. Thirdly, the phenomena by which ESP is characteristically manifested not infrequently have a symbolic quality. Although ESP may take the form of a subject's simply 'knowing' that, for instance, someone has died, and this feeling may not be occasioned by or involve any vivid mental picture, hallucinatory voice calling, or what have you, the information concerned often seems to percolate into consciousness less directly, in the form of inexplicable anxiety, a persistent image, a straightforward dream or hallucination, an obviously symbolic dream or hallucination, or indeed a whole dramatic representation. Thus—and here I am citing actual cases—percipients of 'crisis apparitions' (hallucinations representing some person who is, unexpectedly, at the point of death) may see the phantasms as accompanied by a hearse, as accompanied by Jesus Christ, or as floating up into the sky like Mary Poppins. Now psychopathologists have often suggested that material from the unconscious mind can find its way into the conscious mind only in some disguised and symbolic form; correspondingly, when material which looks as though it may have some symbolic meaning breaks into consciousness, we may suspect that it has emerged from the unconscious.

(c) By far the largest amount of recent experimental work on ESP has been expended in attempts to find conditions or situations which will favour the emergence of ESP, and to discover the personality characteristics of successful subjects. Hypnosis, drugs, meditational techniques, standard personality tests, electroencephalography, biofeedback, emotion-generating experimental materials and many other stratagems have all been made use of in pursuit of these aims. There would, I think, be some degree of consensus among present workers in the field that success in routine ESP experiments is most likely when experimenters are tactful and sympathetic, when subjects are intelligent and imaginative, have outward-going personalities, believe in ESP, and are in a state of tranquil alertness, and when experimental materials have emotive overtones. But it is impossible to force all the findings into a common mould, and they are too numerous to be reviewed in detail. It may, however, be worth looking at one series of consistently successful experiments, namely those of Ullman and his collaborators at the Dream Laboratory of the Maimonides Medical Centre in New York (Ullman *et al*, 1973). From the earliest times it has been widely believed that dream-states are peculiarly favourable to the manifestation of ESP. But such suggestions have been vulnerable to the obvious counter-argument that, since everyone dreams several dreams every night, any reported coincidences between dreams and external events may reasonably be ascribed to chance. Ullman and his collaborators may be said to have provided the first statistical reply to the counter-argument; and they have also, incidentally, produced further evidence that ESP may manifest itself in symbolic form. Most of their experiments have had the following design. In an acoustically isloated chamber lies a sleeping subject, with the electrodes of an electroencephalograph attached to his scalp. In a second acoustically isolated chamber is the 'agent'. Upon receipt of a signal from the experimenter, the agent concentrates upon a picture which he has earlier chosen by means of random numbers from a set of prints, each concealed in an opaque envelope. The experimenter (in a third room), monitors the subject's EEG. When it appears likely that the subject has been dreaming, the experimenter awakens him and records his account of his dream. The records are rated by independent judges for similarity to each of the prints in the evening's set; the subject, too, rates each picture for similarity to his dreams. 'Similarity' here includes symbolic or thematic affinity. Both 'gifted' subjects and volunteers have been used in these experiments, and the majority of results have been significant, sometimes highly so. The successes could be attributed either to telepathy or to clairvoyance, but work has been begun with 'clairvoyant' and 'precognitive' experimental designs.

This completes my brief review of some of the empirical findings which might be thought to have particular relevance to the theoretical understanding of ESP. I shall now pass on to consider the views of two writers who hold that ESP occurs and that we can only understand or explain it if we are prepared to make assumptions of a philosophical kind.

The first of these writers is Professor H. H. Price. In a well-known paper (1949) Price passes from the inadequacies of physical radiation theories of telepathy to the conclusion that 'there is no room for telepathy in a Materalistic universe' and the further conclusion that 'a given mind has direct causal relations . . . with other minds'. The inadequacies of radiation theories will be touched upon shortly, but first we may note that quite a number of other physical concepts have been invoked in attempts to explain ESP (cf. Dean, 1967; Chari, 1974)—for instance gravity waves, world lines, peculiar 'fields', folds in the space-time continuum, extra dimensions of space-time, discontinuities in space-time, hypothetical particles of one kind and another, and even 'mental' energy.

We can divide theories based on such concepts into two broad categories. Firstly there are what may be called 'direct contact' theories, ones which bring agent and percipient or agent and target (or some part or aspect of them) so to speak into spatio-temporal adjunction. Secondly there are mediated contact theories, like the radiation one discussed by Price. These postulate some intervening medium of contact between agent and percipient or between target and percipient.

It is curious that so many of the proponents of these theories seem to think that if they could but give some plausible-sounding account of 'direct' or 'mediated' contact the battle to explain ESP would be all but won.[1] The battle would in fact be hardly begun. It is, to start with, obvious that spatio-temporal adjunction, say of brain with brain or of brain with target, is not a sufficient condition of the occurrence of ESP. There is no evidence that people sitting with their heads together are likely to score highly in telepathy tests. Most of us go through life knowing nothing of the arachnoid membranes in which our brains are encased, nor does a patient in whose brain a bullet is lodged necessarily know more than the next man of the bullet's size, shape, colour, weight and texture. Some kind of relationship other than mere spatio-temporal adjunction must be postulated, and 'direct contact' seems likely to reduce to 'mediated contact', especially since it is hard to see how 'spatio-temporal adjunction' here can be used in other than some non-literal or Pickwickian sense. However, it is equally obvious that the mere occurrence of mediated contact between nervous system and nervous system, or between a nervous system and some object external to it, is no more sufficient for the occurrence of ESP than is direct contact. Cosmic radiation is all the time penetrating one's body without telling one anything about its source; a disintegrated king may go a course through the guts and bloodstream of a beggar without the latter being any the wiser.

I can think of only two ways in which the notion of mediated contact might be developed into a true theory of ESP. The first is as follows. It might be supposed that the medium of contact has imposed upon it by the target object or by the brain of the agent a pattern or property which directly reflects some aspect or aspects of the physical properties of the object or brain concerned, and which so affects the nervous system of the percipient that he is able to adjust, or to learn to adjust, his activities to those aspects of that object or that brain. This gives us an account of ESP closely resembling the accounts we generally give of ordinary sense-perception. I do not see how such an account of ESP can be maintained for a moment. So far as clairvoyance is concerned the problems are highlighted by, though they are not peculiar to, experiments utilising J. B. Rhine's DT (down through) method, a method with which results have often proved seemingly successful. The DT method consists in placing a pack of cards face downwards on a table and asking the subject to guess the identity of each card from top to bottom of the pack. The pack is left undisturbed. Let us imagine, as does C. D. Broad in a classic paper, that the subject is clairvoyantly perceiving the sixth card down. Then on the quasi-perceptual view of clairvoyance :

'We shall have to suppose that the percipient's body is being stimulated by some kind of emanation from the front of the sixth card in the pack, although the back of the card is towards him. We shall have to suppose that the five cards which are on top of the selected one are transparent to this emanation, though they are not transparent to light. We shall presumably have to suppose that the five cards which are on top of this one and the thirty-four which are beneath it (Broad's hypothetical pack has forty cards) are all equally emitting radiations of this kind. Thus the emanation from the selected card will reach the percipient's body mixed up with the emanations from all the other cards in the pack. Next we shall have to assume that, although the emanation is not light, yet there is a characteristic difference between the emanation from the pips and the emanation from the background, correlated with the difference between red-stimulating and white-stimulating light-waves. Without this there is no hope of explaining how the clairvoyant can tell that there are pips and a background and judge the number of pips. Still less could we explain how we can tell the colour of the pips on the selected card. When we look more carefully into the last mentioned assumption we find that it is equivalent to the following supposition. We are, in effect, supposing that the physical difference between the pips and the background, which makes the former selectively reflect red-stimulating light-waves and the latter indifferently reflect a whole mixture of light-waves, is correlated with another physical difference which is concerned with another and unknown kind of emanation. This is certainly not very plausible.'

(Broad, 1953, pp. 38–9)

Broad goes on to deal with the problems raised by the clairvoyant's knowledge of the shape of the pips (imagine, on the visual analogy, the situation where the pack is edge-on), by his ability to pick out from the innumerable radiations reaching him just those which appertain to the sixth card down, by the absence of any distinctive clairvoyant experience, and by the clairvoyant's ability to translate (presumably at an unconscious level) the incoming patternings of the medium of contact into their proper visual equivalents. It is impossible, I feel, not to endorse his conclusion that any quasi-sensory model of clairvoyance must involve 'a very heavy draft on the back of possibility'.

It cannot be said that comparable theories of telepathy involve a draft any less heavy. The objections to 'radiation' theories of tele-pathy are well known : there is no consistent relationship between success in telepathy tests and the distance by which agent and percipient are separated; Faraday cages and other forms of shield-ing appear to have no adverse effect upon scoring rate; and the brain is not known to emit any electromagnetic radiation which would be detectable more than a few millimetres from the scalp.[2] There seem, furthermore, to be some rather more general objec-tions to mediated contact theories of telepathy.

(a) If any form of physical energy transfer be involved, the energy concerned appears not to fall off with distance and to be capable of passing through all human material barriers. But then it should pass through the brain too, and not be stopped as, for example, radio waves are 'stopped' by aerials.

(b) Since *ex hypothesi* the medium of contact is patterned by pro-perties of the agent's brain, the agent's thoughts, if they are to influence the percipient's brain, must be *identifiable* with pro-perties of the agent's brain. This is a notoriously difficult hypo-thesis and any theory which compels it is best avoided if possible. Another debatable assumption to which the theory commits us is that if two people are entertaining the same thought or the same image their brain-states must exhibit the same pattern.

(c) The physiological systems and anatomical loci within which the generation of the patterning may go on, or which may respond to incoming patterns, remain quite mysterious. And I have already remarked on the inadequacies of the popular 'critically poised neurons' theory.

(d) Since all, or at least many, brains must be supposed to be simultaneously patterning the medium of contact in their own ways, including brains as it were in the same 'line' of sight', grave problems once again arise as to how total confusion is avoided, so that, by and large, it is chiefly 'desired' or 'relevant' patterns which affect percipients.

(e) A related problem is this. Consider a case of 'spontaneous' ESP in which a percipient becomes aware that his old friend Fandangle is in anguish. Fandangle's state of mind at the time, i.e. the brain-

state which patterns the medium of contact, could be summed up in the word 'anguish'. His state of mind is not 'I, Fandangle, son of Fandangle, and old friend of the psychically gifted NN, am in anguish'. In other words, what the percipient 'knows' in such cases greatly exceeds anything he can learn from the pattern which the agent has supposedly imposed upon the medium of contact. So far as I can see, only two answers are possible. One is that Fandangle-anguish is somehow distinctively different from the anguish of the other inhabitants of the globe, is, for instance, blended with his own characteristic bodily sensations, thoughts of his unique personal difficulties, etc.; and this simply puts the problem back a stage. The other is to invoke clairvoyance as a supplement to telepathy; but we have already found reasons for strongly suspecting mediated contact theories of clairvoyance.

The second way in which a mediated contact theory of ESP might be developed is this. Upon a patterned medium of contact as defined above might be superimposed a further pattern not directly reflecting the properties of the patterning brain or object, but capable of being 'decoded' to provide information about things other than the immediate source of the patterning. The analogy here is with the communication of information by radio, telephone, laser beam, etc. In the case of telepathy this would presumably involve one part of the brain encoding and 'broadcasting' information about what another part of the brain (the 'thinking' part) or something intimately linked therewith is currently doing. It seems to me that the implications of this theory have only to be spelled out for it to be seen to be grossly implausible. In the first place, it presupposes the existence of a suitable medium of communication and thus falls foul of all the general objections (listed above) to physical theories of telepathy (with perhaps the exception of objection (d), since the 'broadcasting' portion of the agent's brain might utilise a distinctive 'call-sign'). In the second place, the only analogous systems we know of involve processes of deliberate encoding and deliberate decoding by intelligent agents. Now it might be suggested that comparable encoding and decoding systems have evolved in human and animal brains for reasons of biological utility, and that such systems operate outside the sphere of ordinary consciousness. But consider the following points : the code,

although not consciously known to or operated by agent or percipient, must be complicated and flexible enough to transmit information about all the sorts of subject matter that have figured in
cases of ostensible telepathy; it must, like a language, be capable
of encoding messages about novel states of affairs (for we have no
reason for saying that only a few, standard messages can be conveyed by telepathy); and it must be continually enlarged as the
conceptual equipment of the agent enlarges from birth to adult-
hood. So complex a system of communication could have evolved,
one might well argue, only because of its immense biological
utility. Yet, in what does that utility consist? The telepathic system
of communication works spontaneously in man only at the rarest
intervals, and I doubt whether there is any unimpeachable evidence at all for its spontaneous functioning in animals. Furthermore, as Bergson and others have argued, the possession of any
marked degree of ESP might well be a handicap in the struggle
for survival, since it would tend to distract attention from the
exigencies of the immediate situation.

I take it that everyone would agree that no inanimate objects
could have evolved systems for imposing such higher-order patternings on the medium of communication; and that such a theory
of clairvoyance requires no examination.

It appears, therefore, that Price's doubts about the possibility
of a physical theory of ESP have considerable justification, and
this even without adducing the further immense difficulties raised
by the evidence for precognitive clairvoyance and precognitive
telepathy. Should we therefore accept Price's own view that in
telepathy 'a given mind has direct causal relations . . . with other
minds' and perhaps in addition try to develop a 'mental' theory
of clairvoyance? This would involve us not perhaps in accepting
a particular view of the mind-body relation, but at any rate in
ruling out a group of other views. Unfortunately 'mental' theories
of telepathy and clairvoyance suffer from various problems quite
closely analogous to those which beset physical theories. Consider
the telepathy case. Suppose person A concentrates very hard upon
some visual pattern, say a cross, or upon a certain thought, for instance, 'I shall go to London tomorrow', or suppose that his mind
is filled with the deepest despair; then perhaps there might be
manifested a tendency for other persons B. C, D, known to him,

to have an image of a cross, to think of visiting London, or to feel the deepest despair, all without any ordinary reason. Then we might under some circumstances be forced to suppose that A's mental state had somehow induced closely comparable mental states in the minds of B, C, and D. We could say that his mental state had been transmitted to them. But once again we are confronted with the twin questions of how it is that the minds of B, C and D are more likely to be influenced by A's mental states than by the states of some mind, however powerful, which is quite unknown to them, and of how, given that A is influencing their minds, they are able to recognise the influence as his. One could construct all sorts of *ad hoc* hypotheses to cope with these issues, but I see no grounds for supposing that such hypotheses would have greater plausibility than the corresponding ones in the physical case.

Still further problems arise if we take into account the (not infrequent) examples of alleged telepathy in which the correspondence appears to be not between A's mental state and B's mental state, but between A's mental state and some supposed *unconscious* mental state of B's, as for instance when A's mind is apparently influenced by some item of information once known to B, but which the latter is not consciously thinking of and may have forgotten altogether. Some writers have even found themselves forced to suppose that telepathy can take place between A's unconscious mind, and B's unconscious mind.

The problems are no more tractable when we turn to the case of clairvoyance. In fact the main problem, it seems to me, is simply that of arriving at any coherent notion of a purely mental process of clairvoyant perception. This hypothetical process has sometimes been called 'prehension'. The idea seems to be that in clairvoyance what is present to our consciousness is *the object itself*; prehension is thus a direct and irreducible relationship holding between a perceived object, or some aspect thereof, and a percipient mind. This way of talking makes the clairvoyant mind seem rather like an amoeba. It can bypass objects in which it is not interested, and engulf others beyond them in which it is. Again it always prehends the faces of objects (e.g. cards) even though they are sideways on to it so that it has to flow round them. Furthermore (to drop the simile) although prehension can contact (say)

c

an object in a sealed box or the bottom card in a standing pack, it only fixes upon the surfaces of objects, never upon, for example, a level midway through a house wall. Prehension can work on any scale; it can give information about objects the size of playing cards or less; even about the states of electronic circuitry if some experiments be valid; and it can comprehend a house, or a whole hilltop view. Prehension can be functionally equivalent to any given sense modality. In short, prehension can do anything that is required of it; and I cannot form a sufficiently clear conception of the supposed process to be able to examine it further.

The second theoretical approach to ESP which I wish to discuss is the late C. G. Jung's theory of 'synchronicity' (Jung, 1972). Jung holds that ESP and kindred phenomena demonstrate the existence in the universe of a form of order not hitherto explicitly recognised, a form of order which is totally different from the causal order in which scientists and philosophers of science have commonly traded. I will try to give the gist of Jung's position, but I have to confess that not merely am I unable to reconcile different secondhand accounts of his views with each other; I am unable to reconcile different parts of his own writings.

Jung's key notion is that of coincidences which somehow 'make sense' or are 'meaningful'. Such coincidences include all spontaneous and all experimental examples of apparent ESP, but they include also all kinds of omens, whether deliberately sought or otherwise, the hits made by astrologers, scryers, and believers in the I Ching, and all sorts of odd physical phenomena, raps, falling pictures, and so forth, coinciding with deaths or other significant events. These coincidences or correspondences are too numerous to be attributed to the chance harmonising of independent causal sequences—Rhine's experiments have proved that. And furthermore, we cannot give a causal explanation of the coincidences by setting up one of the related events as the cause of the other. For Rhine's experiments have shown that the coincidences are independent of space and also of time, and Jung seems to look upon all 'causal' transactions as involving energy interchanges in a common spatio-temporal setting. Thus 'meaningful coincidences' show that there is in the universe a form of order distinct from the causal.

Flew (1953, pp. 198–9) has objected that Jung's usage of the term 'coincidence is tautological. Coincidences would not be 'coincidences' if they were not meaningful, were not notable in some way. However, I think Jung's coincidences are supposed to make sense or have meaning in a rather special way.[3] They somehow strike those who experience them as symbolising or portending or reflecting events of deep personal or sometimes natural concern, events of a basic and universal kind, birth, death, war, catastrophe, the fate of parents or kings. They may inspire a sense of the numinous, of divine intervention. (Even Rhine's ESP tests had this quality, for successful subjects were greatly impressed by the possible philosophical and religious importance of the experiments.) And in the numinous overtones lies the clue to understanding these phenomena.

According to Jung there lie in our unconscious minds certain basic ways of thought or inherited propensities, ones which are common to the whole human race. These are the archetypes. They never become conscious, but may be represented in our conscious-ness by archetypal images—the great mother, the wise old man, the shadow, the mask, and so forth—each symbolising our in-stinctual attitudes to recurrent human situations. These uncon-scious levels of the personality can somehow transcend space and time, which Jung seems to regard in a somewhat Kantian manner as psychic constructs, and gain or harbour knowledge of spatially or temporally distant events of which the conscious mind could have no inkling. This knowledge is likely to be in some way rooted in or closely linked to the archetypes, and to be about archetypal themes.

Synchronistic events occur when there emerges from the un-conscious an image which either directly represents or else sym-bolises an event whose distant occurrence or whose impending occurrence is already known to the unconscious mind. The event is likely to be of an archetypal kind, so the emergent image will, as it were, have come from the archetype, and will have corres-ponding doom-laden or numinous overtones. Sometimes the un-conscious knowledge may manifest itself not in the injection of an image into consciousness, but by the production in the subject's vicinity of some paranormal physical effect.

It is, however, to be noted that no causal relationship exists between the image and the event which fulfils it. There may be a causal relationship between the unconscious knowledge of the impending event and the emergence of the image, but there can be no causal relationship between the impending event and the unconscious knowledge of it. The unconscious, being independent of space and time, cannot participate in causal relationships, which are essentially spatio-temporal. Consequently, there cannot be any causal relationship between the impending event and the image of it.

This is the most plausible interpretation I can put on Jung's exposition, though I fear it must be inadequate and erroneous in many ways. What are we to say of his views? Many psychologists, (and I am one of them) would be tempted to say that Jung's doctrines about the archetypes are part and parcel of a psychological theory which has dramatic unity rather than logical coherence, and which can therefore accommodate any conceivable turn which the facts may take. Such theories, it might be alleged, are of very little use or interest, for between one such theory and another no decision can be reached except upon aesthetic grounds, and we could go on accumulating these theories more or less indefinitely.

All this may well be true. It seems to me, however, that there is one curious and interesting central idea in Jung's writings on synchronicity which is relatively independent of his speculations about the archetypes, and which is worth pursuing a little further for its own sake. The gist of the idea is this. The term ESP is a complete misnomer. We do not acquire the factual knowledge exhibited in so-called ESP by any quasi-perceptual or transmissive process, though sometimes we may fancy we do because of the form in which it manifests. The knowledge concerned is, from the point of view of our everyday notions of how we acquire factual information, totally anomalous. The knowledge it not 'acquired', the information does not 'arrive'. The knowledge, so to speak, 'happens'. 'However incomprehensible it may appear', writes Jung, 'we are finally compelled to assume that there is in the unconscious something like an *a priori* knowledge or immediate presence of events which lacks any causal basis' (1972, pp. 43–4). I shall now consider, albeit most sketchily, some issues raised by Jung's suggestion that ESP is *a priori* 'knowledge' of empirical facts. I shall touch upon two issues raised for parapsychology, then upon two philosophical issues.

The parapsychological issues are these : firstly, what effects would adoption of this neo-Jungian scheme of things have upon the conceptual framework of parapsychology? Secondly, do we have, or could we obtain, any empirical data which would help us to decide whether or not the neo-Jungian scheme of things is a viable one?

There seems to me little doubt that within the field of parapsychology adoption of these ideas would help to dissolve various problems which have hitherto proved refractory :

(a) We could stop looking for, or thinking in terms of, hypothetical mental or physical processes of transmission or quasi-perception underlying ESP.

(b) We could stop worrying, in connection with precognition about the problem of 'future causes' and all that goes with it. According to my interpretation of Jung, what we have is anomalous 'knowledge' or anomalous true belief concerning future events; and it is not a feature of the concept of knowledge, or of most epistemic concepts, that the event which is known has to be among the causes of the knowledge of it (e.g. I can properly be said to know the date of the next transit of Venus).

(c) Likewise we could stop worrying about whether we can reduce alleged instances of telepathy to clairvoyance or precognitive clairvoyance, alleged instances of retrocognition to telepathy or clairvoyance of contemporary events, and so on, as though our endeavours might simplify the problem of finding some physical or other process of ESP. We all of us do already have knowledge of, and true beliefs about, the past, the present and the future, about external objects, and about other people's minds. To attempt to reduce one of these kinds of knowledge to another would at best be to confuse the 'causes' of knowledge with its 'objects'. For instance, it may well be the case that all one's ordinary knowledge of future physical events is derived from one's knowledge of past or present physical events, so that the latter kind of knowledge is at any rate a necessary condition of the former. But it would be absurd to claim that knowledge of the future is therefore reducible to knowledge of the past and present. To gain knowledge of the past involves exercising (*inter alia*) one's concept of 'pastness', and to gain knowledge of the future involves exercising (*inter alia*) one's concept of 'futurity'; these concepts (whether or not their neural bases, if any, are similar) are different, and exercise of the one is not to be reduced to exercise of the other. In the case of anomalous 'knowledge' there are *ex hypothesi* no causes and the question of 'reduction' *cannot even arise.*

(*d*) A corollary of (*c*) would be this. There appear, as I noted earlier on, to be some instances of apparent telepathy in which there is a correlation not between A's present behaviour or mental state and B's present behaviour or mental state, but between A's present behaviour or mental state and some item of knowledge once possessed by B but not now consciously in his thoughts. There has been a tendency to interpret such correlations in terms of telepathy betwen A's mind and B's unconscious mind. But in terms of the neo-Jungian scheme of things which we are considering we would simply say that A has 'anomalous "knowledge" '—knowledge which is of particular events and yet is not based upon observation or upon inference from observation—of the actual past event known by B. We need not picture him unconsciously and invisibly ransacking B's unconscious mind to disinter the latter's buried memory of that event.

(*e*) If we ceased to think of ESP as a kind of perception or a kind of transmission, we could cease to ask whether the process is mental or physical, and, if the former, whether this empirically demonstrates the independence of mind from matter. The anomalous 'knowledge' exhibited by successful clairvoyants and telepaths need have neither a greater nor a lesser tendency to 'disprove materialism' than does the occurrence of any other form of conceptual activity. Whatever the neural or other processes underlying or constituting propositional thought, ordinary knowledge and anomalous 'knowledge' will alike be manifestations of them.

Whether the conceptual simplifications which adoption of the neo-Jungian scheme of things might introduce within parapsychology would be more than counterbalanced by the general and philosophical problems which it will raise outside it is a further and far more difficult question.

We now come to the issue of whether or not there are, or could be, any empirical data which bear upon the viability of the Jungian position. There are certainly some existing findings which at any rate consort very well with that position. For example :

(a) Among cases of so-called spontaneous ESP, there is a not insubstantial number which take the form of the percipient's simply *knowing*, without any special visual imagery or hallucinatory quasi-percepts, that, for example, something is wrong at home (cf. Rhine, 1961, pp. 63–8; Stevenson, 1970). And between such cases and cases in which there is a fully fledged quasi-perceptual experience it would probably be possible to insert a graduated continuum of cases. We might then find grounds for arguing that the 'knowing' is the basic experience, and that the other forms of experience represent the 'knowings' finding conscious expression in disguised form.

(b) On physical or prehensive theories of clairvoyance and on some 'mediated contact' theories of telepathy, we would expect to find that successful subjects in ESP experiments would have difficulty in discriminating from each other targets or images which physically or qualitatively resemble each other. So far as I am aware, there is little evidence to suggest that this is so.

(c) Analysis of cases of apparent telepathy has suggested to some writers (Rhine, 1961, Ch. 13; Dean, 1967, pp. 38–9) that in such cases the agent is the initiator rather than a passive recipient. This is not easy to account for on radiation and other 'mediated contact' theories, but falls into place if we take the view that in 'telepathy' the agent simply has *a priori* anomalous 'knowledge' of matters that particularly interest and concern him. (Very many spontaneous cases of ESP are about such matters.)

(d) Parapsychologists have not discovered any 'causal laws' of ESP; but they do seem to have hit upon a number of ways of making ESP experiments marginally more likely. Most of these come down to making the subject relaxed and happy. Parapsychologists tend to say themselves that what they are doing here is just facilitating the emergence of the knowledge gained by ESP. They do not claim to be finding out about the actual process of

ESP. This situation would be accounted for if there is no 'process' of ESP.

There are also some existing findings which *prima facie* constitute difficulties for the neo-Jungian position. For example :

(*a*) In some rather striking cases in which series of target drawings have apparently been successfully reproduced by ESP (see especially Sinclair, 1962) the percipient's experience has closely resembled ordinary sense perception. A neo-Jungian would have to suppose that the propositional 'knowledge' presented by the agent amounts to a specification of the physical shape and characteristics of the target, and that this 'knowledge' is exact enough to find expression in a visual image closely resembling the target. It must, however, be borne in mind that a good hypnotic subject can be made, for example, to 'see' as completed the complex patterns of a wallpaper which is in fact interrupted by the presence in front of it of a person made 'invisible' to him. He is able to 'construct' the missing part in great detail from the specifications available to him.

(*b*) Successful experiments on animal ESP obviously pose problems for any view of ESP which makes it essentially a matter of possessing concepts; certainly any experiment which forced one to attribute more than the very simplest notions to a mouse would constitute a grave difficulty.

It is not easy to think of possible lines of empirical work which would decisively discriminate between the anomalous 'knowledge' viewpoint and its rivals, for none of the positions is sufficiently developed to permit exact predictions. The neo-Jungian theory perhaps suggests that success would be likely in some experimental situations in which, according to other theories, it would not be likely. For example, it is probable that many subjects in ESP experiments are constrained by the term 'ESP' and by the experimental materials to regard ESP as some kind of marginal sense-perception. If the neo-Jungian position is valid, their endeavours to summon up quasi-sensory images might actually be a handicap to success. A more appropriate kind of experiment would be one in which, say, they were invited to consider the truth or falsity of propositions, for example about what some person intimately known to them was now doing in another room. Or, if conventional target materials were to be used, they might be so arranged that physical similarity in targets was pitted against what might be called conceptual similarity (e.g. a picture of a pineapple and a picture of a hand-grenade will be physically similar but conceptually different, whilst a picture of a hand-grenade and one of an atomic explosion will be conceptually similar but physically different).

The first of the philosophical issues which I shall touch upon will be mentioned rather than examined. It is that of whether what I have called anomalous 'knowledge' (in scare quotes) is properly called 'knowledge' instead of (perhaps) 'anomalous true belief'. Many philosophers would say that the term 'knowledge' should only be used where the knower has 'good evidence' for what is known. Whether this is so, and whether it might under any circumstances be held that we can have 'good evidence' in cases of anomalous 'knowledge', are questions in which I do not want to become involved. I have used the term 'knowledge' because it seemed the only one which adequately conveyed the percipient's own experience in many cases of apparently spontaneous ESP.

The second philosophical issue I want to touch upon is Jung's claim that synchronistic phenomena represent an acausal form of order. Price (1953, pp. 33–4) has suggested that, in claiming that synchronistic phenomena are not susceptible of causal explanation, Jung may be taking too narrow a view of causality. For Jung a cause and an effect are always two spatio-temporally adjunct objects or events, between the earlier and the later of which there is some kind of energy transfer. But in these post-Humean days we may regard as causally related any two individually identifiable events whose occurrences exemplify a law of constant concomitance. Thus we can relate synchronistic phenomena causally, despite the spatio-temporal discontinuities between them.

This issue reflects upon one which I discussed above; because, to the extent that we reintroduce causal notions into the neo-Jungian's scheme of things, its value in ridding parapsychology of conceptual problems is likely to be diminished.

It seems to me that Price oversimplifies matters somewhat;

which I shall now proceed to do myself, but in a different direction. The situation with regard to synchronistic events appears to be as follows. We start out with a class of events which might be called 'aberrant beliefs'—beliefs as to empirical matters of fact which as it were come upon us without any obvious external or internal causes. A surprising number of these beliefs (the subclass anomalous 'knowings') turn out to be correct. We then try to find some consistent causal connection (e.g. a radiation) between the events of the subclass 'anomalous "knowings" ' and the events which are taken as confirmations of these 'knowings'. We can find no such causal connection. We therefore propose that the confirming events themselves, without any intervening causal connections, be termed the 'causes' of the anomalous 'knowings'. But this is an odd procedure. For the class of confirming events is marked out as a subclass of the class 'events' *only* by the fact that these events confirm anomalous 'knowings'; and anomalous 'knowing's are marked out as a subclass of the class 'aberrant beliefs' *only* by the fact that the 'knowings' are confirmed by the confirming events. Thus the relation between these two classes of events is definitional rather than empirically discoverable. Now this does not *preclude* there being causal relations between the individual events which compose one class, and the individual events which compose the other; any more than a man being a father precludes his having caused the conception of his children. But neither does it *per se* justify us in claiming that there *is* a causal relationship.

It might be suggested that we can in fact propound a weakish law of the following kind. Events of kinds especially interesting or emotionally significant to an agent are more likely than other events to be accompanied by his developing aberrant beliefs. Here the two classes of event concerned—events interesting to an agent and that agent's aberrant beliefs—are ostensibly not related to each other by definition. Nonetheless it seems to me that we do not have a genuine causal law expressing an empirically discoverable relationship between two classes of events. For not any event from one class maybe paired with any event from the other. For example, if I have an hallucination as of seeing my Aunt Jane tumble from the top of the Eiger, this is not verified by the arrival of an unexpected cheque; nor is a dream of an unexpected cheque verified by news of Aunt Jane's demise. Thus the relationship between the class of an agent's aberrant beliefs and the class of the events interesting to that agent consists in the fact that some individual aberrant beliefs (the anomalous 'knowings') each individually correspond to particular members of the class of interesting external events. But what we have here is again simply the epistemic relationship in terms of which the events which await explanation are defined. An epistemic relationship does not necessarily involve, and certainly does not yet amount to, a causal one.

Anomalous 'knowledge' is thus left (on the neo-Jungian interpretation) as an irreducible feature of the universe. What can be meant by talk of a 'general acausal orderedness' or 'form of order' I am not sure. Perhaps the idea is that there are certain fundamental 'categories' or ways of ordering objects or events in relation to each other; and that to such principles of ordering as the spatial, the temporal, the qualitative and the causal, we must add an epistemic principle of ordering not reducible to the category of cause-and-effect. The epistemic category might have ramifications beyond mere synchronicity. These are speculations which I neither wish nor feel able to pursue. But it is perhaps possible that in the end synchronistic *a priori* knowledge will prove as interesting, and every bit as perplexing, to philosophers as synthetic *a priori* knowledge.

REFERENCES

Beloff, J., 'The Place of Theory in Parapsychology', *Research Letter of the Parapsychological Division of the Psychological Laboratory, University of Utrecht* (November, 1972), pp 2–22.

Bierman, D. J. and Camstra, B., 'ESP in the Classroom', in W. G. Roll, R. L. Morris and J. D. Morris (eds), *Research in Parapsychology 1972* Metuchen, N. J., The Scarecrow Press, 1973).

Broad, C. D. *Religion, Philosophy and Psychical Research* (London, Routledge & Kegan Paul, 1953).

Chari, C. T. K., 'The Challenge of Psi: New Horizons of Scientific Research', *Journal of Parapsychology,* vol. 38 (1974), pp. 1–15.

Dean, E. D., 'Parapsychology and Dr Einstein', *Proceedings of the Parapsychological Association,* vol. 4 (1967) pp. 33–56.

Dixon, N., *Subliminal Perception* (London, McGraw-Hill, 1971).

Dobbs, H. A. C., 'The Feasibility of a Physical Theory of ESP', in J. R. Smythies, op cit., pp. 225–54.

Duval, P. and Montredon, E., 'ESP Experiments with Mice', *Journal of Parapsychology,* vol 32 (1968), pp. 153–66.

Flew, A. G. N., 'Coincidence and Synchronicity', *Journal of the Society for Psychical Research,* vol. 37 (1953), pp. 198–201.

Gurney, E., Myers, F. W. H. and Podmore, F., *Phantasms of the Living* (London, Trübner, 2 vols., 1886).

Haraldssen, E, 'Subject Selection in a Machine Precognition Test'. *Journal of Parapsyhcology,* vol. 34 (1970), pp. 182–91.

Hardy, A., Harvie, R. and Koestler, A., *The Challenge of Chance* (London, Hutchinson, 1973).

Jung, C. G., *Synchronicity* (London, Routledge & Kegan Paul, 1972).

Kelly, E. F. and Kanthamami, B. K., 'A Subject's Efforts towards Voluntary Control', *Journal of Parapsychology,* vol. 36 (1972), pp. 185–97.

Koestler, A., *The Roots of Coincidence* (London, Hutchinson, 1972).

Marshall, N., 'ESP and Memory: A Physical Theory', *British Journal for the Philosophy of Science,* vol. 10 (1960), pp. 265–86.

Mundle, C. W. K., 'ESP Phenomena, Philosophical Implications of', in P. Edwards (ed), *The Encyclopaedia of Philosophy* (New York, Macmillan, 1967), vol, 3, pp. 49–58.

Price, H. H., 'Psychical Research and Human Personality', reprinted in J. R. Smythies, op. cit., pp. 33–45, from *The Hibbert Journal,* vol. 47 (1949), pp. 105–13.

Price, H. H., Review of C. G. Jung and W. Pauli, *Naturerklärung und Psyche, Journal of the Society for Psychical Research,* vol. 37 (1953), pp. 26–35.

Rhine, L., *Hidden Channels of the Mind* (London, Gollancz, 1961).

Schmidt, H., 'Precognition of a Quantum Process', *Journal of Parapsychology,* vol. 33 (1969), pp. 99–108.

Schmidt, H. and Pantas L., 'Psi Tests with Internally Different Machines', *Journal of Parapsychology,* vol. 36 (1972), pp. 222–32.

Sinclair U., *Mental Radio* (Springfield, Illinois, Thomas, 1962).

Smythies, J. R. (ed.), *Science and ESP* (London, Routledge & Kegan Paul, 1967).

Stevenson, I., 'Telepathic Impressions: A Review and Report of Thirty-five New Cases', *Proceedings of the American Society for Psychical Research,* vol. 29 (1970), pp. 1–198.

Targ, R and Hunt, D. B., 'Learning Clairvoyance and Precognition with an ESP Teaching Machine', *Proceedings of the Parapsychological Association,* vol 8 (1971), pp. 9–11.

Thouless, R. H., *From Anecdote to Experiment in Psychical Research* (London, Routledge & Kegan Paul, 1972).

Ullman, M., Krippner, S. and Vaughan, A., *Dream Telepathy* (London, Turnstone Books, 1973).

NOTES

(1) A theorist who does not make this assumption is Marshall (1960). Marshall holds that any two physical things exert upon each other an

'eidopoic' influence, whose effect is to make them more alike. This influence is stronger in proportion to (a) the complexity of structure of the objects concerned and (b) their existing similarity of structure. Only the human brain is complex enough in structure to exhibit this effect to an appreciable extent, and it manifests it in telepathy. I do not think, however, that this theory of telepathy can be taken seriously. Many instances of apparent spontaneous telepathy involve knowing what is going on in someone's mind; this is quite different from one's mind becoming like someone else's mind. Furthermore, we have so far reported instances of, for instance, parent–child telepathy. Can we really suppose that there is likely to be a sense of 'similarity of structure' in which a mother's brain is more similar in structure to her young son's than it is to that of any adult, living in her street?

(2) Dobbs (1967) has argued that the first of these objections may be overcome in various ways. But he apparently accepts the others; and it can hardly be denied that it would be a great boost to radiation theories of telepathy if telepathy showed signs of obeying the inverse square law.

(3) Under the influence of Jung, Arthur Koestler has, like a latter-day Aubrey, indulged in the wholesale collection of coincidences of (apparently) any sort whatever (Koestler, 1972; Hardy, Harvie and Koestler, 1973) and has concluded that they may exemplify an integrative tendency by which the universe evolves order out of randomness. Since I cannot regard the majority of his cases as anything other than straightforward coincidences, there is no point in my trying to decide whether the conclusion is justified.

2

THE METAPHYSICS OF
PRECOGNITION

by

BOB BRIER

Precognition, as all other parapsychological phenomena, fails to conform to our traditional world schema. Because of this non-conformity, philosophers such as C. W. K. Mundle[1] have tried to demonstrate that the very idea of precognition involves contradictions, and critics such as C. E. M. Hansel[2] have tried to demonstrate that precognition experiments are the result of fraud and error.

Instead of rejecting the notion of precognition out of hand for its lack of conformity, it might be more fruitful to re-examine and, in some cases, revise some aspects of our traditional world schema. In this paper I will re-examine three concepts and, in two cases, suggest revisions that would accommodate precognition : determinism, causality and space-time.

DETERMINISM

It is often argued that one of the philosophical implications of precognition is determinism. That is, if someone can by precognition know what I am going to do before I actually commit the action, it appears as if I am determined to do that act. For example, if a psychic who is extremely proficient at predicting the future predicts that I will go to the cinema tomorrow night, and if he is always correct, it seems as if I have no choice but to go to the cinema. (It is true that there are no psychics who are perfect predictors, but for philosophical argument we can imagine one.) The determinist will tell us that it is merely the illusion of choice that I have; I merely think I can decide whether or not to go to the cinema. Since this is an event that seemingly can be precognised, and consequently the psychic can know even before my 'decision' whether or not I am going to the cinema, then I really have no choice; it has already been determined.

Those arguing for determinism frequently cite case studies to show the impossibility of avoiding a precognised event. Indeed, it is true that at times people frantically try to avoid the fate that has been precognised for them and fail. An example of this is the case of Robert Morris Sr, the father of the financier of the American War of Independence. Morris had a precognitive dream in which he saw himself being killed at sea by a cannon. He was to visit a ship, but decided to cancel the visit in order to avoid this fate. The captain, however, convinced Morris to come aboard on the proviso that he would not fire the cannon in salute until Morris was safely ashore and out of range. After the visit Morris was being rowed ashore. The captain fully intended to keep his word, but a fly landed on his nose, he scratched his nose, and his men took this as the signal to fire the cannon. Part of the discharge of the cannon hit Morris and killed him.[3] Here the determinist is quick to point out that the very act of trying to avoid his fate seems to have brought about that fate. He will further point out that 'precognition' is a success word. It is not possible to precognise an event that does not eventually happen. Thus, once one admits that Morris's experience was precognitive, one is committed to admit that he had to be killed at sea.

There is an obvious rejoinder to the determinist. What follows from the fact that Morris's dream is precognitive is not that he *must* be killed at sea but merely that he *will* be killed at sea. But this does not mean that he *must* be killed at sea and it is this stronger position that the determinist needs to prove. It seems quite possible that there are several actions that Morris can take to save his life. They are real possibilities—he merely makes the wrong choice. When a predictor foresees my future action, it is quite possible that he is precognising the result of my free choice of one of the possibilities open to me.

Here I might point out that if the determinist's logic were

valid, he would not even need precognition to prove determinism. The logic is precisely the same as presented by Aristotle in his famous case of the sea battle.

(1) Either there will or will not be a sea battle tomorrow.
(2) If there will be a sea battle tomorrow, then nothing I can do can prevent it.
(3) If there will not be a sea battle tomorrow, then nothing I can do can start it.

There is nothing I can do to either prevent or start a sea battle tomorrow.

Aristotle has two false premises (the second and third) that lead to his deterministic conclusion. What he should say is 'If there will be a sea battle tomorrow, then nothing I *will* do *will* prevent it.' He, like the determinist arguing from the assumption of precognition, is assuming what is to be demonstrated. From the fact that an event *will* occur it simply does not follow that it *must* occur.

From the treatment above it is clear that this kind of argument falls far short of deriving determinism from precognition. Consequently, in this instance, precognition has no metaphysical import. There is no suggestion as to whether our world is a deterministic one or one allowing for freedom of the will. However, a completely different kind of argument has recently appeared which, although it does not mention precognition explicitly, involves determinism, and could be used to show that precognition is logically impossible, since it leads to a contradiction. The argument is far more compelling than any of the other arguments against the possibility of precognition, and an analysis of the argument even leads to a suggestion of what concepts about our world might have to be revised to accommodate precognition.

CAUSALITY

Newcomb's paradox was devised in 1960 by William A. Newcomb, a theoretical physicist at the Lawrence Laboratory of the University of California, Los Angeles.[4] The paradox involves a choice one must take.

There are two boxes labelled I and II. Box I has $1,000 in

it, and Box II has either $1,000,000 or nothing. The $1,000 in Box I is visible, but Box II is covered. The money is placed in the boxes by a Being who has the remarkable ability to predict which of the two options you will exercise. You may choose either the contents of the covered box only or the contents of both boxes. If, however, the Being predicts that you will take both boxes, he places nothing in Box II. If he predicts that you will take the contents of Box II only, then he places the million dollars in it. What is your strategy? There are compelling arguments for each of your options.

(a) It is obvious that you should select the contents of Box II only, since the Being will have predicted your choice and consequently have placed the million dollars in it. (Had you selected both boxes the Being would have predicted that and left Box II empty.)

(b) It is obvious that you should select the contents of both boxes. The Being has already made his predictions and either placed or not placed the million dollars in Box II. Nothing is going to change whether there is or is not the million dollars in Box II, so you might as well take the contents of both, have a chance at the $1,001,000, and have nothing to lose at this point by such a decision.

Nozick gives a lengthy decision theory analysis of the problem and concludes that one should take both boxes. He does not solve the problem, however, but merely gives one kind of analysis which yields a course of action. Nozick realises this, and at the end of his paper he calls for more satisfying solutions from others. The first to oblige were Maya Bar-Hillel and Avishai Margalit.[5] They find Nozick's decision theory analysis unsatisfactory and offer their own. There is little point in discussing such analyses in this paper. These kinds of formalisms may provide one with a reason for exercising one option rather than the other, but they do not explain why one feels in such a bind when presented with the two options. Only a conceptual analysis will do this, and in an attempt to get at the crux of the problem Bar-Hillel and Margalit provide this also.

D

The problem, they say, may not be which strategy to choose, but whether there could possibly be such a Being. Can anyone rationally believe that the Being has, prior to one's choice, made His prediction and either placed or not placed the million dollars in Box II, and also believe that the probability of receiving the million dollars is dependent upon which strategy one now picks? If one believes that 'there can't possibly be such a Being' (here we might point out that the Being is basically a precogniser, and thus the issue reduces to whether or not precognition is logically possible), the paradox has no bind and one obviously takes both boxes. But there is no clear logical contradiction involved in the existence of such a Being. Bar-Hillel and Margalit come to the conclusion that one should take only Box II. But their specifying which choice they would take does not resolve the paradox. They merely give a directive for action. Of their strategy they say, 'It is not justified by arguing that it *makes* the million dollars more likely to be in that box, although that is the way it appears to be, but because it is inductively known to correlate remarkably with the existence of this sum in the box, and though we do not assume a causal relationship, there is no better alternative strategy than to behave as if the relationship was, in fact, causal' (p. 303).

Like Nozick, they too have merely presented a course of action (in this case based on induction), but have avoided the real issue. They realise that the paradox centres around the amazing cor- relation between the earlier events of the Being's prediction and placing or non-placing of the million dollars in Box II, and the later event of your selection of one or both boxes. The authors are hesitant to call the correlation causal, and this is understand- able, for if it is causal, there are two alternative descriptions of the situation, and neither is appealing : (1) It might be that the Being's prediction or placing of the money in the box in some mysterious way causes you to choose in accordance with his prediction. If this is the case, then you have no real choice but are determined to 'choose' the way he predicts. (2) It could also be that your choosing causes the Being to make his prediction and subsequently either place or not place the million dollars in the second box. In this case, backward causation would be involved.

In a detailed analysis, it will be seen that the situation described by Newcomb is not contradictory and consequently quite possible. It is true that one at first sees both arguments (the inductive one for the Being's ability to predict, and the deductive one leading to the suggestion that one take both boxes) as compelling, and thus one does not know whether to take one or both boxes. However, the deductive one is not valid. The resolution of the paradox lies in realising that backward causation is possible, and this points out the invalidity of the deductive argument for taking both boxes. In another work,[6] I have shown that those who thought they had demonstrated the logical impossibility of a cause coming after its effect were in error, and thus here I will discuss only the import of the possibility of backward causation for Newcomb's paradox.

The way we view the situation is that the choice of one or both boxes causes the Being to make his prediction and consequently either place or not place the million dollars in Box II. Thus what you do after the money is in the box (or is not in the box) is what brought the situation about. It is wrong to think that at the moment of your choice the money is either in the box or not in it and consequently nothing you can now do can affect that. True, the money is either in the box or not, but this might be because of the choice you now make! With this in mind, it is clear what your decision ought to be. Since the later choosing causes the money to be placed in Box II, you ought to take only Box II, since this assures that you will get the million dollars. Otherwise you will definitely have only the thousand dollars. It should be noted that this interpretation allows for free will. We can now view the Being as one who precognises the result of your free choice of alternatives.

It should be pointed out that this is not the only way of resolving the paradox. As noted earlier, it is possible that the Being's predictions cause your choice. In this case the Being may have free will, but you certainly do not. If this is the case, there is again no real paradox; here you merely think you have two choices but really do not have any choice.

We have seen that the resolution of Newcomb's paradox lies in the rejection of the deductive argument for taking both boxes. One is left with two ways of viewing the situation—one involving mysterious forward causation between the Being's predictions and your choices, and a perhaps even more mysterious backward causation where your choice determines the earlier prediction. In the first case there is no real course of action, since your 'choice' is determined. In the second it is obvious that you should take the contents of Box II only. Which of these two alternatives is preferable is not clear. However, by examining a less bizarre case, we might gain support for one of the two alternatives.

Consider a standard precognition test in which a subject predicts which of the five ESP symbols (star, waves, circle, square or plus) will be selected the following day by a random procedure. If the subject repeatedly scores significantly above chance, we may be justified in believing that there is a causal connection between the guesses on one day and the actual order of the symbols on the following day. Which causes which? It is possible that the guess causes the selection of symbols in some mysterious way. It is also possible that by backward causation the selection of the symbol causes the subject to have guessed that particular symbol. We could check to see if the process of selection is in fact random. (We could do this by checking the symbols generated for patterns or indications of nonrandomness.) If it is random, a possible conclusion is that it was unaffected by the guesses, and it is the guesses that are caused by the symbols selected. This is not airtight, but it is the kind of evidence that might help to decide which of the two options to select. We might also consider spontaneous cases of precognition.

If a psychic precognises a plane crash which in fact occurs on the following day, we again might wish to say that there is a causal connection between the plane crashing and the precognitive experience—but which caused which? Here, to me at least, it seems more likely that the plane crashing caused the precognitive experience rather than the precognitive experience causing the crash. Even if we knew of the precognition, we would still look for the cause of the crash. We would search the wreckage for signs of metal fatigue, an improperly hatched door, etc. Thus we might locate the cause of the crash, but we must still locate the cause of the precognition. It would seem to be the crash. So we have some evidence for choosing backward causation as our description as opposed to the equally mysterious forward causation.

The point to be emphasised here is that Newcomb's paradox did not demonstrate the impossibility of there ever being such a predictor, nor did it demonstrate the impossibility of precognition. Rather, because the assumption of precognition led to a seeming contradiction, we were forced into an analysis of causality, which led to the suggestion of backward causation. Actually, in another article[7] I tried to show that the concept of *causality* as we now use it does not specify temporal priority of causes over effects. Thus a conceptual revision is not really necessary; all we need is a realisation that there is nothing in our universe that prohibits a cause from succeeding its effect. Indeed, precognition may suggest that this is the case.

SPACE-TIME

The traditional view of the universe is that of a four-dimensional manifold : the three dimensions of space (height, depth and width) and time constitute our physical world. Formerly, the temporal dimension was the one most discussed among philosophers. However, just before the turn of the century, mathematicians such as Reimann, Lobachevsky and Bolyai challenged the idea of space being necessarily Euclidean, and this has led to wider speculation about the properties of our physical universe. In this section I will examine the possibility that we in fact do not live in a world in which there are three dimensions of space, but in one in which there are four, time being the fourth spatial dimension. The purpose of this exercise will be to see if such a notion can be of help to us in accommodating the phenomenon of precognition.

Although the mathematicians mentioned above did not deal with the geometry of higher dimensions, they stimulated considerable thought in this area. One of the most forceful proponents of a fourth-dimension theory was C. Howard Hinton who published *The Fourth Dimension* in 1904.[8] Hinton's approach was championed and carried a little further by the Russian mathematician P. D. Ouspensky.[9] It is interesting to note that both men mix mysticism and wild speculation with their geometrical treatment of the fourth dimension. Probably for this reason their treatment of the higher dimension aspect, which is basically sound, is to a great extent overlooked by serious philosophers and metaphysicians. I believe, however, that although they were not attempting to explain precognition or revise our metaphysics to account for such phenomena, a careful re-examination of this possibility might do just that.

The immediate problem of postulating that we live in a world with four dimensions of space is that we have no means of knowing or imagining what that fourth dimension is, or where it is. Thus we run the risk of literally not knowing what we are talking about. One way to solve the dilemma is to imagine what lower dimensional beings (those who live in one-, two- or three-dimensional worlds) might perceive, then try to imagine ourselves in a similar dilemma.

We might begin by imagining a one-dimensional creature who lives on a line. All his experiences would consist of moving along his line. As he passed through point after point his experiences would change. He would, of course, have no concept of right or left, all he could know would be forward or backward. Any two-dimensional object would be experienced only in one dimension. Though the two-dimensional object is made up of infinitely many one-dimensional cross sections, our creature would not be able to imagine this. If he came across a square it would not be perceived as being being made up of infinitely many lines; it could be perceived only as a line. Needless to say, our creature who has no conception of the second dimension would also have no idea of the third.

We might now go on to a two-dimensional creature. We can imagine that he lives on a plane and has complete mobility on that plane. However, he cannot perceive the third dimension—he has no concept of up or down. Unlike his one-dimensional counterpart, he can perceive a square on his plane. He can not, however, perceive (or conceive of) a cube. If there were a cube going through his plane he could only experience the points where the cube intersects the plane, and would see a square, though not all at once of course. Since we are examining what it would be like for lower-dimensional creatures to live in higher-dimensional worlds so that we might get a feeling for what situation we might be in if in fact our world does have four spatial dimensions, it might be instructive to examine one experience in the two-dimensional world in detail.

Imagine that there is a two-dimensional being who lives on Plane ABCD (Fig. 2–1).[10] Periodically, a horseshoe magnet is lowered through his plane. The magnet is in four sections, each having a different pattern. What will our being perceive?

Obviously he has no conception of up or down. Thus he will not be aware of the presence of the horseshoe magnet. All he will be able to experience is that portion of the horseshoe that intersects with his plane. If he explores, he will discover two squares. Now let each pattern on the magnet represent different colours. The blank portion is white, the horizontal stripes are green, the vertical

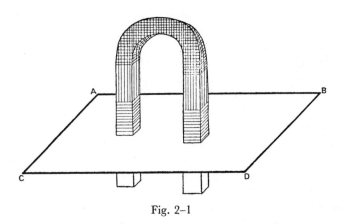

Fig. 2–1

stripes are blue and the checked portion is red. Since the magnet is lowered periodically, the two-dimensional being will perceive that the squares change colour periodically. But he might say something additional if asked. If we ask him about the white squares he will tell us that they were there once but changed to green. If we ask him where the white squares are he will tell us that white is no longer: 'It doesn't exist any more.' 'It is in the past.' But it is not in the past. It still exists in the *third* dimension of space. Because he cannot perceive the third dimension of space, he makes an error in time. For him red is in the future and white is in the past, while they actually still exist simultaneously in the third dimension of space. If for a fleeting moment, the two-dimensional being were permitted to look up and report to a friend what he saw, he might describe seeing blue, and then when blue intersected with the plane he might be called a psychic for having seen the 'future'. If he were repeatedly allowed to look up, he could consistently predict the future. The crucial point here is that when he would be described as having seen the future he would merely be seeing the present (third dimension). To the inhabitants of the plane it would be inexplicable how our being could know the future. Such abilities would not conform to their known laws of physics.

This temporal problem of theirs is not unlike the situation in which we three-dimensional beings find ourselves. Frequently we come across people who apparently see the future. At rare times we come across an individual who has several such experiences and seemingly can predict the future with regularity. This too does not conform to our known laws of physics. What I am suggesting is that we might be in a similar situation as our two-dimensional friend, only one dimension higher. We might be living in a four-dimensional spatial world and are normally able to perceive only three of these dimensions and consequently make errors in time. We think that yesterday is gone and tomorrow is not yet, but they may both exist now, in the fourth dimension of space. Analogous to the example of the magnet going through the plane, if each colour were a different season of the year, the two-dimensional being would mistakenly think summer is gone and winter is to come. We too think that the seasons follow one another temporally. But they might all exist simultaneously in four-dimensional space.

This revising of our spatio-temporal schema does, to some extent, bring our way of viewing our universe into accord with the facts. There are, however, problems. One immediate drawback is that such a view does not explain how one is at times permitted to catch a glimpse of the fourth dimension of space. I do not have an answer to this problem, but perhaps an answer could be formulated. There is another problem. We have been talking about four-dimensional space but have not really delineated any of its properties. How are we ever to work out a comprehensive theory if we do not know any of the properties of what we are talking about? There are some things we can say about the fourth dimension, but they will have to be derived by analogy with the lower dimensions.

Firstly, we know that the second dimension is at right angles to the first and that the third dimension is at right angles to the first and second. Thus we can specify that the fourth dimension is orthogonal to the first three dimensions. This is not very much, but it is a start. Secondly, we know that each lower dimension is a cross section of the next higher one. A point is a cross section of a line; a line is a cross section of a plane; and a plane is a cross section of a cube. Thus our three-dimensional world would be a cross section of a four-dimensional one, and we might expect a four-dimensional object to be composed of an infinite number of three-dimensional objects. Again, this is only a start, but it indicates the way in which we might eventually piece together enough information to develop new hypotheses as to the nature of our universe.

There is no question that the concept of precognition does not conform to our ordinary world view. Either our way of viewing the universe is incorrect, or those who feel they have accumulated evidence for precognition are mistaken, deluded, deceived, etc. Because I believe the evidence is sufficiently strong to establish the existence of precognition, I am interested in seeing how our traditional views might be revised.

In this paper I have tried to show briefly how such an analysis might be begun on three concepts: determinism, causality and space-time. I have tried to show that precognition is actually compatible with either determinism or freedom of the will, and have suggested revisions of the concepts of causality and space-time that would accommodate precognition.

The preliminary analyses of the concepts of causality and space-time were intended merely to show how philosophers might contribute positively to the work of parapsychologists who are searching for a theory that will guide research. By revising concepts until a coherent comprehensive description of the facts is possible, we may be able eventually to formulate a psi theory. It is quite possible that there simply are not yet enough data to guide the development of a theory. But we must start sometime.

58   PHILOSOPHY AND PSYCHICAL RESEARCH

REFERENCES AND NOTES

(1) C. W. K. Mundle, 'Does the Concept of Precognition Make Sense?' *International Journal of Parapsychology,* vol. 6 (1964), pp. 179–98.
(2) C. E. M. Hansel, *ESP: A Scientific Evaluation* (London, Charles Scribner's & Son, 1966).
(3) Ian Stevenson, 'Precognition of Disasters', *Journal of the American Society for Psychical Research,* vol. 64 (1970), p. 193.
(4) Robert Nozick, 'Newcomb's Problem and Two Principles of Choice', in *Essays in Honour of Carl G. Hempel,* ed. N. Rescher et al. (New York, Humanities Press, 1970), pp. 114–46.
(5) Maya Bar-Hillel and Avishai Margalit, 'Newcomb's Paradox Revisited', *British Journal of Philosophy of Science,* vol. 23 (1972), pp. 295–304.
(6) Bob Brier, *Precognition and the Philosophy of Science* (New York, Humanities Press, 1974).
(7) Bob Brier, 'An Atemporal View of Causality', *Journal of Critical Analysis,* vol. 4, no. 1 (April 1972), pp. 8–16.
(8) C. Howard Hinton, *The Fourth Dimension* (London, Sean Sonnenschein & Co., 1904).
(9) P. D. Ouspensky. *Tertium Organum* (New York, Vintage Books, 1970).
(10) The author acknowledges his thanks to Miss Judith Turner for drawing the illustration to his paper.

3

ESP AND THE MATERIALIST
THEORY OF MIND

by

DAVID E. COOPER

I

Materialism, it would be fair to say, has been the most flourishing
of recent philosophies of mind. A host of philosophers—especially
from the antipodes—actively embrace it;[1] and many others, if
not actually committed to it, espouse a view of mind which is at
least compatible with a materialist one, and which they expect
to be converted into a materialist one in the light of further
scientific discoveries.[2] Furthermore—and this is a sure sign of
how a theory has flourished—writers in areas outside of philosophical psychology frequently presuppose a materialist account
of mind, and take compatibility with such an account as a con-
straint on adequate analyses of whatever it is that occupies their
interest.[3] In this paper, I want to look at a question which
materialist philosophers rarely mention and even more rarely discuss : the implications for their position of the claims of parapsychology. Cynics would say that materialists dare not discuss such
a question. In particular, I shall assess the assumption—the near-
universal assumption—that if the claims of parapsychology can
be made out, materialism must be rejected. This assumption, I
shall argue, is mistaken.

It is only with psychological materialism, with materialism considered as a philosophy of mind, that we shall be concerned. There
is a more general doctrine of materialism, which denies that any-

thing non-material exists. Abstract entities such as Classes are ruled out by this doctrine, but we shall only be interested in the ruling-out of non-material minds. Unfortunately there is no single version of psychological materialism. However, the version to have attracted most attention over recent years has been some brand or another of the so-called 'Mind/Brain Identity Thesis'. As its title suggests, the Thesis holds that, while there are mental events (states, processes, etc.), these are strictly identical with physiological or neurological events etc. occurring in the central nervous system. There are not, therefore, two types of events, mental and physical, standing in some form of correlation to one another: rather, psychological descriptions are of precisely the same events as certain physiological ones are. The descriptions, of course, are correlated, in the sense that a certain physiological description will be true when, and only when, a certain psychological one is true. However the descriptions are not of correlated, distinct events, but of identical ones. Indeed, the reason the descriptions correlate is that they describe precisely the same thing. Identity theorists typically stress that the identity in question is of a purely contingent or empirical kind. Our physiological talk in no way resembles our psychological talk in meaning. If it did, we could establish materialism simply through semantic analysis. In fact, establishment of it depends upon empirical success in the sciences of neurology and physiology. This success would include finding, for each type of psychological description, some type of physiological description that is true when, and only when, the first is true. The identity is, therefore, more like the empirically discovered one between water and H_2O than that between the class of bachelors and the class of unmarried men.

It is with the Identity Thesis that we shall be mainly concerned. It is worth mentioning, though, that a seemingly alternative version of materialism has won favour in some circles—the so-called 'Eliminative Materialism'.[4] On this view, it is not that there are mental events (which happen to be identical with brain ones); rather, there are no mental events at all (only brain ones). Our ordinary talk of pains, beliefs, or desires, it is argued, is analogous to primitive talk of demons or miracles. We do not say, nowadays, 'There are demons, and these are identical with viruses', but instead, 'There are no such things as demons; the illnesses primitives thought were caused by demons are in fact viral'. Similarly, it is suggested, we ought not to say, 'There are pains, and these are identical with brain events' but, 'There are no such things as pains; what were wrongly referred to as pains are simply brain events'. On the eliminative view, our psychological talk embodies a fallacious immaterialist theory which will disappear with the introduction of a proper physical one. Our psychological talk will then be swept away along with the old theory. I shall not, except where necessary, refer to the 'eliminative' version, for not only are the respective merits of the two versions unimportant for the purposes of this paper, but the whole of my defence of the Identity Thesis in the face of ESP could, with suitable alterations, serve as a defence of the 'eliminative' version as well.[5]

I am going to make a number of large assumptions about materialism in the present paper. Firstly, I assume that the required correlations between psychological and physiological descriptions will be established, that a wide range of statements like 'A person is in pain if and only if his brain is in condition X' will be verified. In other words, I take it that neurologists and physiologists are going to be as successful as materialists hope. Secondly, I assume that materialists can satisfactorily cope with a whole host of conceptual objections that have been levelled against their thesis. For example, I take it that an objection like the following can be dealt with : descriptions by a person of his own mental states are sometimes incorrigible in the sense that he could not be mistaken in them (e.g. 'I am now in intense pain'), whereas no physiological descriptions could be similarly incorrigible : hence psychological and physiological descriptions cannot be of the same events, for if they were, the events would be ones about which we both could and could not be mistaken.[6] (Actually a materialist can tolerate some of the conceptual objections against identifying the mental and the physical provided he switches to some brand of the 'eliminative' version. For if our usual ways of talking about the mental are not coherent, then there will be no obligation to reconcile physiological talk with these ways. See note 5 also). Finally, I assume that certain very high-level, methodological principles that materalists typically appeal to are indeed acceptable. In particular, I accept that on principles of simplicity and economy materialism ought to be embraced, if, on logical and empirical grounds, it can be embraced. It is simplar because it postulates fewer kinds of entities, and, probably, fewer kinds of laws.

The assumptions I have just made add up to the grand assumption that materialism is an acceptable theory of mind—*unless the claims of parapsychology show it not to be*. My interest is not in the general pro's and con's of materialism, but in the specific question of whether it must be rejected because of ESP, even if it is acceptable on all other grounds.

The term 'ESP' will be interpreted in a strong way. A mental event will count as extra-sensory only if, in some suitably substantial sense of 'physical', it is incapable of being explained in physical terms. ESP phenomena will not be strange ones that are very difficult to explain within the framework of physical laws; they are ones which cannot be explained at all within that framework. Naturally it would be difficult to spell out the suitably substantial sense of 'physical' referred to. On the one hand we would want to avoid an over-narrow definition that equated 'physically explicable' with 'explicable within physics as it now stands', for clearly genuine extensions of physics may explain tomorrow what physics cannot explain today. On the other hand we want to avoid an over-generous definition which will allow us to call any explanation we ever produce a physical one. (Chomsky has said somewhere that the issue of whether everything is scientifically explicable is in danger of being a vacuous one, because of the tendency to stretch the word 'science' to cover any theory we happen to be satisfied with.) Luckily I think I am able to ignore what an appropriate sense would be by adopting the following manoeuvre. At any point in the history of materialism, the materialist must be employing the term 'physical' in some substantial sense. If he is not, the claim that mental events are identical with physical ones becomes vacuous. Let us now say that events are to count as extra-sensory, at any given time, only if they are incapable of being explained in physical terms in whatever sense of 'physical' the materialist is at that time employing in his theory. Such an account introduces a perhaps unwelcome temporal element into the question of whether events are to count as extra-sensory. But it captures what is, for us, the crucial point that extra-sensory experiences cannot be regarded by the materialist as explicable in physical terms. For, in whatever sense of 'physical' he is employing, extra-sensory events will be precisely those that are not physically explicable. The purpose of ensuring this result, of course, is to see what is *special* about the problem ESP creates for materialism : If ESP phenomena are allowed to be ones which the materialist simply thinks difficult to explain in physical terms, they provide him with no special problem. My way of characterising 'physical' guarantees that from the materialist's own standpoint extra-sensory experiences always provide a special case.

My comments on how 'ESP' is to be taken have the consequence, perhaps, that one could never know if ESP occurs; for could a person know there were experiences incapable of explanation within a proper extension of his framework of physical theories? Still, it seems to me that a person could have good reason to think that ESP occurs; good reason to think that no theory sufficiently analogous to his present physical theories to warrant the unequivocal title of 'physical' could cater for certain phenomena. This, it seems to me, is a desirable consequence.

There is just one assumption I want to make about extra-sensory experiences (given that they occur)—namely that significant correlations between their occurrence and the occurrence of certain events in the central nervous system can be established.[7] I assume, in other words, that statements of the kind 'A person is having a telepathic experience of what someone else is feeling if and only if his brain is in state X' will be found to be true. There is no reason to think this assumption any more implausible (or plausible) than the corresponding assumption made in connection with normal experiences. After all, if a person is having a telepathic experience he is in *some* brain-state, and why should the brain-states not be similar when the experiences are? This seems to me just as likely or unlikely as that a man should be in similar brain-states each time he enjoys the taste of a banana. The reason I make this assumption is, once more, in order to focus upon what is special about the problem ESP creates for materialism. Now failure of significant correlation between *any* kind of mental event and some kind of physiological event would put paid to materialism.[8] Actually, as we shall see, it is not on such grounds that critics have thought materialism threatened by ESP. Certainly the *confidence* with which materialism is asserted to be incompatible with ESP would be misplaced if the whole case rested on the unlikelihood of such correlations being established.

It is time to illustrate what I have referred to a number of times—the near-universal assumption that materialism and the claims of parapsychology are incompatible. H. H. Price writes:

'. . . the implications of telepathy are . . . incompatible with the Materialistic conception of human personality . . . telepathy is something that ought not to happen at all, if the Materialist theory were true. But it does happen. So there must be something seriously wrong with the Materialist theory, however numerous and imposing the *normal* facts which support it may be.'[9]

Price, of course, is a well-known critic of materialism. But when we turn to that arch-materialist, David Armstrong, we find the same assumption being made. After considering possible physical explanations of alleged paranormal phenomena, he writes: '. . . if these ways of escape prove unsatisfactory, Central State Materialism cannot be the whole truth about the mind . . . (ESP is) the small black cloud on the horizon of a materialist theory of mind.'[10] Price and Armstrong differ only in their beliefs concerning the likelihood of ESP. For Armstrong, ESP is only a '*small black cloud*' because he is pretty sure there is no such thing. But anti-materialist and materialist alike seem to agree that *if* ESP occurs then materialism must be false.

II

The assumption referred to and just illustrated has tended to precisely that—an assumption. Perhaps the incompatibility is considered too obvious to require argument. Still, I think one can glean from various writings what the underlying argument would be. It would take the form of a *reductio ad absurdum* of the materialist hypothesis. Let the first premise be a simplified statement of that hypothesis:

(*a*) Each mental event is identical with some physical event.

Let the second premise be the apparently plausible following claim (which I shall refer to as the 'physical explanation claim'):

(*b*) All physical events are explicable in physical terms.

Let the third premise be the asumption that ESP occurs :

(c) Some mental events—i.e. extra-sensory experiences—are not explicable in physical terms.

A contradiction is easily derived from these three premises. The contradictory conclusion is that some mental events both are and are not explicable in physical terms. That they are not is what we are told by (c), and that they are follows from (a) and (b) (for, if any mental events is a physical one, and any physical one is explicable in physical terms, then any mental event is similarly explicable). So the assumption of materialism has resulted in a contradiction. Hence, if ESP is assumed to occur, materialism must be given up. More informally the argument is this : given there are mental events inexplicable in physical terms, and given too that what is truly physical must be so explicable, then the mental events cannot be physical ones. It is clearly some such argument that underlies Sir Cyril Burt's judgement that 'the utter failure of all purely physical hypotheses (to account for the paranormal) . . . leaves the door wide open for a psychical or mentalist hypothesis'.[11]

Actually, even if the argument forces us to withdraw (a), all we are obliged, strictly speaking, to give up is the materialist account of extra-sensory experiences, for we are not obliged to conclude that no mental events are physical. It would not follow, in other words, that the materialist's treatment of normal experiences is mistaken. Still, while this does not follow, it could reasonably be argued that once certain mental events are admitted to be non-physical in kind, none should be treated as physical. It would seem implausible to suppose that extra-sensory experiences differ from the normal not only in their causes but also in, so to speak, the medium or substance of their occurrence. The very same principle of economy that materialists appeal to would suggest that if we are anyway forced to admit non-physical mental substance then we should make do with that alone. At any rate I shall take it that if we are forced to give up premise (a) at all, it is the materialist treatment of mind in general that is mistaken.

But are we forced to give it up? Let us look more closely at the argument. Like any *reductio* argument, it forces us to reject one premise but not any one in particular. The contradiction

E

could equally well be avoided by withdrawing premise (c). However, we do not want to do that since (c) represents the working
assumption of this paper—that ESP occurs. So it is only (b)—the
physical explanation claim—that we might reject instead of (a),
to avoid contradiction. Now I am not going to discuss whether
the physical explanation claim is true or even plausible. I do not
need to, since I can show something else which is more to the
point: namely that unless (a) is true the physical explanation
claim cannot be true. In other words, if we reject materialism we
must also reject the view that all physical events are explicable in
physical terms. (This is so, whether or not we entertain ESP.) If
I am right, the argument against materialism is incoherent, for
it relies *inter alia* on acceptance of the physical explanation claim.
But it is impossible to accept that and to reject materialism.
Hence one cannot use the truth of the claim as a premise for
rejecting materialism. Or put it like this. We could avoid the
contradiction by simply giving up (b) instead of (a). If someone
says, 'But wouldn't it be better to give up (a) rather than (b)?', the
reply to him is that it is impossible, once (a) is given up, to retain
(b). Since a *reductio* argument forces us to give up at least and *at
most* one premise, the argument considered forces us to give up
only (b), the physical explanation claim.

I shall now defend my assertion that acceptance of the physical
explanation claim entails acceptance of materialism. I hope I
will be granted the following:

(i) John's sudden fear of falling off the bridge is a mental event;
(ii) John's splashing into the water below the bridge is a physical
event;
and
(iii) John's sudden fear of falling off the bridge might be the
(partial) cause of his splashing into the water a few moments
later. (His fear made him giddy, which made him slip, which . . .
etc. . . .).

If the physical explanation claim is true, then John's splashing
into the water, since it is a physical event, must be explicable in
physical terms; its causes must be physical ones. Since one of the
causes is John's sudden fear, then this too must be a physical
event. If it is not, and if it really is a cause of the splash, then the

splash is not explicable in purely physical terms, and the physical explanation claim is false.

Here is another example. I hope I will be granted the following :
(i) Mary's telepathic awareness of what her brother is feeling is a mental event;
(ii) The perspiration of Mary's hands is a physical event :
and
(iii) Mary's telepathic awareness might be the (partial) cause of her hands' perspiring. (Frightened by her realisation of her strange powers Mary became nervous, which made her hot . . . etc. . . .).

It will be impossible to accept that the perspiration was physically explicable—impossible, therefore, to accept the physical explanation claim—unless one also accepts that Mary's telepathic awareness was a physical event. If it was not, the perspiration would have had a non-physical causal antecedent. Generalising from such examples, we can say this : none of the physical effects of mental events (normal or paranormal) would have explanations in purely physical terms unless the mental events are physical ones. In other words, the physical explanation claim is true only if materialism is true.

At least two objections might be raised against what I have been saying. It might be urged, first, that a statement like 'John's sudden fear caused his splashing into the water' is really elliptical for something like 'John's splashing into the water was caused by physical events in his central nervous system that were correlated with his sudden fear'. If so, we can hang on to the physical explanation claim without embracing materialism, since there is no reason to suppose the mental event correlated with the physiological cause is itself a physical one. This objection amounts, in effect, to an admission that mental events do not really have physical effects, that statements like 'John's fear caused the splash' or 'Mary's awareness caused the perspiration' are never literally true. This admission seems to me, frankly, to be too high a price to pay for retaining the physical explanation claim while rejecting materialism. In the first place, we do ordinarily take it that statements like the ones above can be literally true. We do think that it is pains, fears, and desires themselves which can have physical effects. Secondly, mental events, if they do not really belong in causal sequences, become just the 'nomological danglers' materialists have accused them of being; events whose postulation is useless for explanatory purposes. Our objector cannot have it both ways. He cannot hold both that mental events play a genuine explanatory role and that the physical explanation claim is true. Either they do play such a role, in which case the physical explanation claim is false unless we treat them materialistically. Or the physical explanation claim is true, in which case the effects do have sufficient physical explanations, and the mental events become 'danglers' unless they are treated materialistically. Assuming the objector would not be happy with the second option, his defence of the physical explanation claim crumbles.

A second objection might run as follows : 'Your argument to show that rejection of materialism entails rejection of the physical explanation claim relies on taking as physical events—John's splash, Mary's perspiration—ones which have been caused by mental ones. And you go on to conclude that unless the latter are treated as physical, the former will not have explanations in physical terms. But with what warrant do you take John's splash or Mary's perspiration as physical events? Is it not part of our very understanding of what counts as a physical event that it should be explicable in physical terms? To the extent that it is doubtful whether an event was caused by purely physical antecedents, to that extent it is doubtful whether it was really a physical event.' What is being driven at here is that the physical explanation claim is something of a tautology. If 'physical event' means *inter alia* 'event explicable in physical terms', then the claim is necessarily true and, as such, not threatened by the *reductio* argument we are assessing. Hence only premise (a)—the materialist thesis—remains as the argument's victim. It will be no use my saying that if materialism goes so must the physical explanation claim, for I shall be told that I am begging the question in favour of materialism; for my arguments have depended on taking certain events as physical which, it is now alleged, they will not be unless it is question-beggingly assumed that their mental causes are physical in nature. For—to repeat the objection—events are only properly regarded as physical if their causes are physical.

It seems to me that the proposal to regard events as physical only if their causes are physical is misplaced. A complete examin-

ation of this proposal would doubtless involve detailed examination of the precise criteria for calling an event 'physical'—a
task, I suspect, that other contributors to this volume might be
undertaking. Fortunately I think I can bypass such an examination and still be in a position to reject the proposal or, at any
rate, to discount its relevance as an objection to what I have been
saying. In the first place, any account of what it is for an event
to count as physical must, in the absence of *very* strong arguments to the contrary, respect our paradigm applications of the
expression. Now if a body falling into water or a hand perspiring
are not proper examples of physical events, I am not sure what
are. Such events are among the paradigms of what we apply the
term 'physical' to. I can certainly be in serious doubt, for one
reason or another, whether winning a race, making a promise,
getting married, or coming to a decision are physical events. But
I find it difficult to be in similar doubt about bodies falling or
hands perspiring. We seem perfectly happy to count these and
other events as physical, quite irrespective of what we consider
—if we have considered at all—the causal genesis of them to be.
There is nothing peculiar, I suggest, in the question, 'Did that
physical event have a physical cause, or indeed any cause at all?';
and nothing of a self-contradictory air about the statement, 'That
physical event had no cause at all, physical or otherwise.' In the
second place, it is not clear that the position of the physical
explanation claim *vis-à-vis* materialism would be substantially
altered even if the proposal in question were accepted. The
materialist, surely, does not classify brain events or events in the
nervous system as physical in virtue of their being caused by
other physical events (though, very probably, he assumes they
are). He classifies them as physical in virtue of whatever criteria
for being physical he might be employing. I do not, I have said,
want to get involved in the question of just what these criteria
might be—though I should guess they would include at least
the following : applicability to events of *precise* spatial and temporal descriptions, and the absence in the descriptions of any
essential, irreducible reference to social conventions. (It is because
we are not sure what sense can be attached to precise locating of
a marriage—does it take place in the church, in the area before
the altar, on the exact spot the couple are standing upon, or

what?—and because we are doubtful if all reference to social convention can be eliminated in our description of a marriage, that we are uneasy about counting a marriage as a physical, or *merely* physical, event.) Whatever grounds the materialist might have had for classifying events as physical, he will still have those grounds after the proposed legislation which restricts the word 'physical' to events known to have physical causal antecedents. Hence he will have grounds for employing a new predicate— 'physical*', say—in just the way he used to employ 'physical'. 'Physical*' will differ from 'physical' in not entailing that the events to which it applies have sufficient explanations of a physical sort. The materialist's claim will now be that all mental events are physical*. Mental events, that is, are held to have all and only the characteristics of physical ones, except, possibly, that of having physical causes (or any causes at all). The relevantly reformulated physical explanation claim will then be that all physical* events are explicable in physical terms. Thus reformulated it remains, as it surely should, a non-tautologous, substantial claim. It will also remain, therefore, a possible victim of the *reductio* argument. And my insistence that it must be a victim, and must be rejected if materialism is rejected, remains unaffected.[12]

It will be useful to spell out just what I have and have not tried to establish in this section. I have not established that materialism ought to be retained in the face of ESP, that there would be any point or merit in retaining it. I have established, I hope, that it *can* be retained. We are not, that is, logically constrained to reject it in order to avoid contradiction. The *reductio* argument forces us to give up one premise, to be sure, but that premise can be the physical explanation claim. Since this claim would *anyway* have to be given up if materialism is, it would, from a logical point of view, be an unnecessary 'overkill' to give up materialism as well as the claim. All that ESP forces us to admit is that certain events cannot be explained in physical terms. It does not force us in addition to say that the events in question are non-physical ones. For all that has been shown so far, there is no clear advantage in saying that extra-sensory experiences are nonphysical ones for which we have no explanation rather than that they are physical events of an extraordinary type. No doubt it would come as a rude shock to someone of a materialistic bent to find that there are events inexplicable in physical terms. But, logically, there is no reason why the whole of his shock should not be absorbed, so to speak, by giving up the physical explanation claim, thereby leaving his basic hypothesis intact.

III

It is one thing to show that materialism can, without offence to logic, be held on to by a parapsychologist. It is quite another to show that there would be any point in doing so, any good reasons for it. Indeed, an apparently strong line of argument can be presented for saying that, in a world in which ESP occurs, materialism would have none of the value and plausibility it may have in a more humdrum world. It might run as follows :

'Materialism derives its whole impetus and rationale from the assumption that physical events and states will be discovered to occupy the same positions in various regularities as mental events and states have been taken to occupy. Only then could it be reasonable to identify the mental events with physical ones or to eliminate them in favour of physical ones. For the materialist, our understanding of a mental event is an understanding of the regular and characteristic ways in which it is brought about, and of the regular and characteristic effects—especially behavioural —it has. Our idea of pain, for instance, is that of something which is brought about in characteristic ways like damage to the skin, and of something which regularly brings about such behaviour as screaming, wincing or complaining. In Armstrong's words : "What we mean when we talk about the mind, or about particular mental processes, is nothing but the effects within a man of certain stimuli, and the cause within a man of certain responses."[13] It is only if physical events and processes could have the same causes and effects as the mental ones that identity between them can be asserted. For instance, if no physical state could be discovered that had the same sorts of causes and effects as pain does, then we could not identify pain with any physical state.

Now once ESP is allowed, the materialist programme founders. *Ex hypothesi* extrasensory experiences are not governed by the regularities of the physical world. One could still insist that the experiences themselves are physical events, but there would be no point in doing so. For the whole point of identifying experiences with physical events is that, by doing so, one gives them a place in the causal regularities of the physical world; and these, the materialist assumes, are the only regularities we need for purposes of explanation or prediction. It will be no good saying that unless we identify experiences with physical events they become 'danglers' outside of our laws; since, in the case of extra-sensory ones, they would remain 'danglers' even if they were identified with physical events, for the physical events, by definition, would not be explicable in terms of physical regularities.'

We could bring the argument into closer connection with the discussion of the last section. Rejection of the physical explanation claim, we saw, did not force us to give up materialism as well. But, it is now being argued, once that claim is rejected there could be little or no point in retaining materialism, for the claim provides the materialist with the rationale and faith for his hypothesis. Once it is admitted that various mental events cannot be explained in physical terms, then the purpose one had in reducing the mental to the physical is lost. The reduction will no longer result in the placing of mental events within the framework of physical regularities, the network of physical explanations.

There is no doubting the power of this line of argument for rejecting materialism in the face of ESP. Nevertheless I am not convinced by it. At the very least one should consider certain lines of resistance before accepting its conclusions. I shall make three resistant replies, in increasing order of importance.

(*a*) If we do insist on treating extra-sensory experiences as physical events, in spite of everything, it is not clear how our position is any worse than that of various other theories, in other areas, which have not been thought absurd (even if, for one reason or another, they have fallen out of favour). I have especially in mind what is often referred to as 'emergentism' in biological theory. An emergentist, I take it, holds that certain biological phenomena cannot in principle be explained or predicted on the basis of physical laws (laws, in this context, known to or embraceable by physics). Of course he does not deny that the phenomena themselves are, in a perfectly acceptable sense, physical ones. What could be more physical than, say, the presence of certain bacteria in a liquid? What are denied the status of physical are the laws governing such occurrences and states of affairs. Instead, special 'emergentist' laws are postulated. There is some parallel here to the position of the materialist *vis-à-vis* paranormal mental events : they are physical events not subject to physical laws. It is true that in recent years emergentism has lost the popularity it once had; but its decline has resulted from advances in physical theory. Phenomena once thought recalcitrant to physical explanation have been found susceptible to it. Spontaneous generation, for example, seems largely falsified. Now no similar reason is going to be found for rejecting the materialist account of extra-sensory experiences, since these are by definition not susceptible to physical explanation. It would seem to me, then, that materialism is no worse off than a theory like emergentism in biology, and nor is it liable to a similar kind of refutation.[14]

(*b*) Now for a more important consideration. Philosophers and nonphilosophers sympathetic to parapsychological claims tend to react, in their attitudes towards mind, in one of two directions. Some see ESP as validating a certain philosophy of mind alternative to materialism. Others retreat into a pessimistic mood in which all theory is suspended; the mind is regarded as something too mysterious to capture. Yet others, unfortunately, think they are doing the first when in fact they are doing the second. They proclaim some doctrine vaguely referred to as 'immaterialism' or 'spiritualism' or 'psychism', which, incompatible with nothing, is devoid of any substance. Rather than dupe others and themselves, by using these labels, into thinking a genuine theory is being offered, they would do better to admit cleanly they have no idea what mind in a world of ESP is like.

If we are not going to retreat into pessimistic suspension of all theory—and I don't think we should—materialism, it seems to me, is no worse off than the alternatives people have jumped at. Burt writes that, with materialism rejected, Cartesian Dualism is the philosophy of mind most congenial to the parapsychologist.[15] Another author, Mundle, prefers Berkeleyan Idealism as the view most in harmony with ESP.[16] I doubt, though, that Descartes' and Berkeley's doctrines are any happier bedfellows of ESP than materialism. Of course, if 'Cartesian Dualism' or 'Berkeleyan Idealism' are being used, simply, as pretentious titles for any view incompatible with materialism, or for no view at all, then we have not been presented with any specific, assessable alternative suggestions at all. In what follows I shall assume that the labels are being employed with some historical accuracy.

Consider, first, the Cartesian form of Dualism. For Descartes, a mind is a distinct substance whose features enter into two types of regular connections. Firstly, there are regular and direct connections between the various psychological states of any given mental substance. My pain, for example, is regularly and directly connected to my desires, intentions and the like. Secondly, there are regular and direct connections between the psychological states of some mental substance and the physical states of the particular body in which it is 'lodged as a pilot'. When my foot gets damaged, I regularly and without coincidence feel pain. Such an account contains no admission of their being direct, regular, noncoincidental connections between the states of one mental substance and those of another, or between the states of a mental substance and the physical states of a body other than the one in which it is 'lodged'. If such connections were admitted, Descartes could not have had the reason he did for treating a mind as a distinct mental substance; and if he had not treated the mind in that way the result would simply not be Cartesian Dualism. I do not know if Cartesian Dualism is strictly incompatible with ESP. I doubt that it is. What I am more sure of is that the facts of ESP cannot, so to speak, be any more congenial to a Cartesian than to a materialist. Any problems ESP might cause for the notion of mind as brain are also problems for the notion of mind as distinct mental substance.

Consider, next, Mundle's suggestion that the parapsychologist might find Berkeleyan Idealism his appropriate philosophy of mind. The aspect of Berkeley's theory that apparently appeals to Mundle is the claim that the regularities 'governing' mental events are merely divinely ordained correlations. They are statistical regularities which we can observe among the events God has willed to occur. That a person is, in general, only aware of what is happening in the vicinity of his body is one such regularity. But, given His versatility, there is no reason why these regularities should be strict; why, for example, there should not be the occasional person whose awareness is not correlated with what is happening in the vicinity of his body, but with what is happening in the vicinity of his distant brother's body. On this view, the only difference between extra-sensory awareness and normal awareness is the rarity of the former. The connection between the awareness and what it is awareness of is simply that of divinely ordained correlation. Now it seems to me that the only aspect af Berkeley's thought to which essential appeal is being made, in order to make ESP look unproblematical, is a certain theological aspect. The *Idealist* aspect—the denial of material substance—is neither here nor there. Now there is nothing to prevent the materialist appealing to the same theological aspect. If the crucial point is that connections between mental events and other mental or nonmental events be regarded as divinely ordained correlations, it is irrelevant to insist that the mental events are necessarily nonphysical in nature. Why should it not be said that connections are divinely ordained correlations between physical events (including those which can also be counted as mental ones)? ESP phenomena then become statistically unusual correlations between certain physical events, and nothing more than that. Someone might say, of course, that a materialist is hardly able to appeal to God in explanation of anything. Well, certainly the general materialist (see p. 59) can have no place in his universe for God, but there is no incompatibility between theism and the assertion that the minds of natural creatures are physical in kind. (I personally know one religious materialist, and no doubt there are plenty of others in the history of philosophy. Hobbes?) Anyway, although I said earlier that Mundle's position appeals to a theological aspect in Berkeley's theory, it is not obvious that it has to. For perhaps the essential point is simply that causal connections are to be thought of in a certain way—as mere statistical correlations that might hold between any sorts of events at all (including, say, my thoughts and your bodily processes). The doctrine that these correlations are as they are because of God's will then becomes inessential. While this is a dubious view of causal connection, it is not one that only the anti-materialist is permitted.

Naturally I cannot consider here how each reasonably specific and respectable alternative to materialism fares in the face of ESP. But on the basis of the examples I have taken and others I have in mind, my feeling is that no such theory is likely to fare any better. There is a rather general reason, too, why this should be so. Any philosophy of mind is bound to have been founded upon the normal, indisputable behaviour of the mind. It was the normal phenomenon of memory, and the normal interaction of a mind with just one body, for instance, that suggested and constrained the Cartesian doctrine of distinct mental substances. Extraordinary phenomena—whether of the ESP variety, the 'thinking robot' variety, or many others[17]—are almost bound to require adjustments, at the very least, to any such theory. Precisely because a philosophy of mind will, quite correctly, have been tailored primarily to encompass and explain normal, undisputed psychological facts, ESP is almost certain to disturb it.

(c) So far—as, no doubt, will have been noted—my 'defence' of materialism has been negative. It is not logically incompatible with admission of ESP; it is no worse off than analogous theories in other areas; it fares no worse than various alternative philosophies of mind in the face of ESP. But, it will be said, I have not dealt with the particular objection raised at the beginning of this section; and, to the extent that I have not, would it not be wisest, given my other points, to retreat into that pessimistic suspension of theory referred to earlier? Fortunately, I think I am able to deal with that objection. It ran, remember, something like this: the materialist understands a mental event as that which is brought about in certain characteristic ways and which, in turn, has characteristic behavioural effects. Only if physical events having the same causes and effects could be discovered would it be justified to identify the mental events with physical ones; for it is only then that we would prevent the mental events being 'danglers' by identifying them with physical ones. ESP shows, though, that there are mental events which do not belong in the sort of causal chains to which physical events could belong, for they are not brought about in accordance with physical laws. To identify the extra-sensory experiences with physical events would simply result in making the physical events 'danglers' outside laws. Hence there could be no point in making the identification.

The objection involves attributing to the materialist the view that understanding a mental event is to understand *both* what brings it about *and* what it brings about. Now I have no quarrel with the second half of this attribution, but I do with the first. The view can, admittedly, be attributed to Armstrong, as we see from the quote on p. 71. But even he, elsewhere, relegates our understanding of what characteristically brings about mental events to a subsidiary position.

'The concept of a mental state is primarily the concept of a state of the person apt for bringing about a certain sort of behaviour . . . it is the cause of behaviour. In the case of some mental states only they are also states of the person apt for being brought about by a certain sort of stimulus.'[18]

And certainly other materialists ignore altogether the causes of mental events or states in their analyses of psychological concepts.[19] Whatever particular materialists might have said, I think it would be a mistake to include reference to such causes in these conceptual analyses. It is just not true, I think, that our understanding of what a kind of mental state is—pain, say—necessarily involves knowledge of what characteristically brings it about. I have no time, I am afraid, to defend this assertion at length; but I will say this: wherever it seems that identification of a mental event entails reference to its causes, the identification is never *simply* of a mental event. It is arguable that 'He saw a dog' entails that his experience was brought about in a certain way—by the presence of a dog in his visual field. But for just that reason we might deny that 'see', in such contexts, refers solely to psychological occurences. We might contrast 'He saw a dog' with something like 'He had a visual experience as of a dog', allowing only the latter as a 'pure' psychological description. Now this description, surely, entails nothing as to how such experiences are typically brought about. Substitute 'pink rat' for 'dog', and there is no temptation to think such an experience is typically brought about by the presence of a certain animal. Alcohol, caffeine or hypnosis are just as likely.

At any rate, I hope you will grant me—for the duration of this paper—that the materialist need not and should not include reference to characteristic causes of mental events in his analyses of psychological concepts. It follows that materialism derives its whole thrust from the assumption that physiological states or events will be discovered having just the behavioural effects analytically ascribed to certain mental states or events.[20] And it follows that it is in a world in which behaviour could not be seen as the effect of physiological states that materialism would lose its rationale.

It is now obscure how extra-sensory experiences create the problem for materialism that, according to the objection being considered, they are supposed to. The peculiar difficulty of ESP is not with what behaviour extra-sensory experiences result in, but with what it is that brings them about. If the sort of example which would deprive materialism of its point is that of a mental event whose behavioural consequences could not be those of any physiological one, then extra-sensory experiences do not, as far as we know, provide that sort of example. Of course, it might turn out that no physiological states are significantly correlated with extra-sensory experiences, or that the physiological ones could not have the behavioural consequences attributed to the experiences. But this seems to me no more probable than the same thing turning out in connection with ordinary experiences. If the proper analysis of belief involved reference to how beliefs are typically brought about, and if, as would be the case with those extra-sensorily acquired, some could not have been brought about in accordance with physical laws, then indeed there could be no point in identifying them with physical states. By doing so we should not have prevented the beliefs 'dangling' outside a self-sufficient framework of laws. But if we see the purpose of materialism to be, simply, allocation to the mind of a genuine role in explaining behaviour, then that purpose is not thwarted by the parapsychologist's claims.

A count of heads would show, no doubt, that few materialists take the possibility of ESP too seriously. In some cases this may be because of the fear that it would be incompatible with the materialism they find so attractive. More likely it is because the general picture of the universe that the sort of person attracted to materialism has formed has no room for ESP. This suggests —and who would want to deny it?—that the parapsychologist's faith contrasts with the faith, the world view, of one drawn towards materialism. But I deny that those who grasp, in the face of ESP, for alternative philosophies of mind are likely to find themselves in any happier a position. And I deny that materialism loses its thrust and purpose once the paranormal is admitted.

NOTES

(1) See, for example, H. Feigl, 'The "Mental" and the "Physical" ', *Minnesota Studies in the Philosophy of Science*, vol. 2 (1958); J. J. C. Smart, 'Sensations and Brain Processes', *Philosophical Review*, vol. 68 (1959); and D. M. Armstrong, *A Materialist Theory of Mind*, (Routledge & Kegan Paul, 1968).

(2) Noam Chomsky, for instance, has pointed out that while, given the specific anti-behaviourist purposes of his picture of the mind, it is indifferent whether the mind be thought of as a neurological, spiritual, metallic, or rubber substance, the first is the most likely candidate.

(3) See, for example, Hartry Field's discussion of the constraints imposed by physicalism on definitions of Truth. 'Tarski's Theory of Truth', *Journal of Philosophy*, vol. 69 (1972).

(4) See especially R. Rorty, 'Mind—Body Identity, Privacy, and Categories', *Review of Metaphysics*, vol. 19 (1965).

(5) Actually the two versions do not present us with a clear-cut Either/ Or. Some philosophers have opted for a hybrid materialism incorporating aspects of both the Identity Thesis and the 'eliminative' version. Smart has recently argued that while we could not reasonably object to the 'hard core' of our psychological talk, we need not accept all our usual ways of talking about the mind as coherent. "Further Thoughts on the Identity Theory', *Monist*, vol. 56 (1972).

(6) For this objection, see K. Baier, 'Smart on Sensations', *Australasian Journal of Philosophy*, vol. 40 (1962).

(7) For the materialist, strictly speaking, the correlations are not between the mental and physical *events*, but between their descriptions (as explained on p 60).

(8) Though see J. Kim for comments on the precise relevance of these correlations for materialism. 'Phenomenal Properties, Psychophysical Laws, and the Identity Theory', *Monist*, vol. 56 (1972).

(9) 'Psychical Research and Human Personality', in *Science and ESP*, ed. Smythies (Routledge & Kegan Paul, 1967), pp. 36 and 38.

(10) Ibid., p. 364.

(11) 'Psychology and Parapsychology', ibid., p. 119.
(12) The proposal may have got some of its point from certain ways of speaking we have. For instance, we sometimes divide behavioural disorders into physical and psychological (or psychosomatic) ones according, apparently, to whether they have physical causes—like a brain tumour—or not. Still, the sense in which it may be denied that a disorder has a physical cause is surely not meant to exclude the possibility that, in another sense, it does have a physical cause. When it is said that a psychosomatic disorder has no physical cause, what is being denied, I should think, is that it has an *obvious* physical cause like a brain tumour. It would be rash to rule out the presence of some unobvious cause of, say, a biochemical sort.
(13) Ibid., p. 79.
(14) Naturally I would not want to exaggerate the affinity between emergentism and materialism. For one thing it is difficult to see how anyone could want to deny that the relevant biological phenomena are physical, whereas it is only too easy to see why people should want to deny that mental events are physical. Some philosophers have, parenthetically, wanted to draw a strong parallel between the mind and emergent biological phenomena, treating psychological properties as ones that have emerged, in physically unaccountable ways, in advanced neurological systems. Armstrong, op. cit., discusses this view.
(15) Ibid.
(16) 'The Explanation of ESP', in *Science and ESP*, op. cit.
(17) I am thinking, particularly, of how the possibilities of brain transplants, etc., opened up by advances in surgery and neurology, disturb traditional ideas on personal identity and hence the mind. See, especially, D. Parfitt, 'Personal Identity', *Philosophical Review*, vol. 80 (1971).
(18) Armstrong, op. cit., p. 82.
(19) For example, D. Lewis, 'An Argument for the Identity Theory', *Journal of Philosophy*, vol. 63 (1966).
(20) Incidentally, I do not want to be taken as defending the claim that psychological concepts are fully analysable in terms of the behavioural effects of mental events and dates. Elsewhere, indeed, I have criticised that claim—though I have my doubts about what I then said. (See 'Materialism and Perception', *Philosophical Quarterly,* vol. 20 (1970).) My present point is simply that they are not to be analysed in terms of the causes of mental events and states.

4

THE SOURCES OF SERIALISM[1]

by

ANTONY FLEW

I

It is now over forty years since Gilbert Ryle first proclaimed to
the Aristotelian Society his own reluctant conversion to what was
later to become a quite widely shared view about the main if not
the only proper business of philosophy. Philosophy is, or ought
largely to be, 'the detection of the sources in linguistic idiom of
recurrent misconceptions and absurd theories.[2] I shall not, however, consider this general thesis about philosophy here. Instead,
I propose to examine one particular example; and to do this without prejudice to any such sweeping questions about the nature,
or the true nature, of that discipline which I too am with Ryle
paid to profess. The example to be examined is an example of an
absurd theory. It is an absurd theory, the main sources of which
in fact lie in, and can be convincingly identified as, picturesque
idioms. Yet, despite warnings from its author, it is in all probability taken most often not as a philosophical exercise, but as a
contribution to the science, or the would-be science, of parapsychology.

The theory is that propounded by J. W. Dunne in his book
An Experiment with Time. This book was first published by A.
& C. Black in 1927. It went into a second edition in 1929. A dras-
tically revised and extended third edition was published by Faber
& Faber in 1934. Page references will be to this. I myself first read
the book at school along with all my sixth-form contemporaries,

F

although I only acquired my own copy of the third impression of January 1935 secondhand in 1949. Faber put the book into paperback in 1958, and new impressions are apparently called for pretty constantly. This publishing and personal history is worth mentioning. For it shows that Dunne's theory deserves some critical attention as a very minor social phenomenon, quite apart from whatever may be due to its intrinsic interest and merit.

II

The book itself contains two kinds of material: the first, observational and experimental; the second, theoretical. Dunne was led by a series of ostensibly precognitive experiences to devise an experiment. This consisted in recording all his dream-material immediately on waking up. Later he looked for elements which he could interpret as precognitive in this dream-material.[3] He came to believe that he had discovered that precognitive dreams are common, and that his results would be confirmed by anyone repeating his experiments. This crucial claim of repeatability does not in fact seem to have been made good. In 1932, for instance, Mr Theodore Besterman, as Research Officer for the Society for Psychical Research in London, conducted three series of tests: firstly, with a group of SPR members aged about 45–50; secondly, with some Oxford undergraduates; and, thirdly, with Dunne himself. The results were not impressive.

But my concern here is only with the theory. Dunne called this theory Serialism. The name is appropriate. For the gist of the extremely complicated view expounded in *An Experiment with Time*, and elaborated later in *A Serial Universe*,[4] is that there must be an infinite series of time dimensions. This infinite series still has, in spite of its infinity, a last term: 'At infinity we shall have a Time which serves to time all movements of or in the various fields of presentation. This time will be *"Absolute Time"*, with an absolute past, present, and future.' Furthermore, in order to observe any events we need an 'observer at infinity' (p. 186: italics and capitals original). Dunne hastens to reassure us, ' "Observer at infinity" does not mean an observer infinitely *remote*, in either Time or Space. "Infinity" here refers merely to the number of terms in the series. The observer in question is merely your ordinary, everyday, self, "here" and "now" ' (p. 188 : italics and capitals original).

Stripped down thus to the bare bones, this theory is manifestly preposterous. In its full elaboration of complexity the absurdity is far harder to detect. C. D. Broad, however, early and unerringly put his finger upon the fundamental fallacy. He wrote, 'If I thought, as Mr Dunne seems to do, that I should have to postulate an unending series of dimensions and then an "observer at infinity" (who would plainly have to be the last term of a series which, by hypothesis, could have no last term) I should of course reject this alternative as nonsensical'.[5]

These are harsh words, but to the point. Broad's criticism here is shattering and decisive. No elaboration of complications can possibly save Dunne's theoretical edifice from complete collapse. For the series of time dimensions cannot be infinite if it is to have a last term. What the expression 'infinite series' means precisely is 'a series which goes on indefinitely'. By definition, therefore, such a series cannot have a final term. It is no use trying to reassure us by explaining that the 'observer at infinity' is perfectly homely and harmless, because he is 'our ordinary everyday self'. Such assurances may conceal the fundamental contradiction. They cannot remove it.

Since Dunne's position is thus fundamentally incoherent, and indefensible, it is not necessary to investigate all its ramifications in detail. It will, for instance, be sufficient merely to mention that Dunne thought that his views entailed all sorts of portentous consequences 'of considerable importance to mankind' (p. 5). 'Serialism discloses the existence of a reasonable kind of soul—an individual soul which has a definite beginning in absolute time, a soul whose *immortality, being in other dimensions of Time, does not clash with the obvious ending of the individual in the physiologist's Time dimension* . . . It shows that the nature of this soul and of its mental development provides us with a satisfactory answer to the "why" of evolution, of birth, of pain, of sleep, and of death' (pp. 235–6 : italics and capitals original). After making several further claims of this sort, the author modestly concludes: 'A theory which can achieve all this is not lightly to be set aside' (p. 237).

These claims call merely for mention, not for examination. For

if the premises from which such conclusions are supposed to follow
are themselves not defensible, then it is superfluous to inquire
whether or not it is possible validly to infer these conclusions
from these premises. As a matter of fact it is not possible. For how
could we validly deduce conclusions about the existence or the
nonexistence, the mortality or the immortality, of such putative
incorporeal substances as rational souls; from premises which
make absolutely no mention of anything but dimensions of time
—whatever these may be?

III

Our problem is different. It is : How was Dunne misled into this
strange and ill-starred theory, with its flagrant and irreconcilable
contradictions? In view of the facts that he devoted a large part
of his book to descriptions of ostensibly or at least allegedly precognitive dreams, and that he had put a great deal of hard pioneer
work into investigating such dreams, it might be thought that
Dunne's Serialism was not merely encouraged by, but somehow
grounded upon, the alleged occurrence of ostensibly precognitive
dreams. But Dunne himself emphasises the contrary : 'The reader
will note, I hope, that the foregoing tenets of Serialism have *not*
been deduced from the empirical evidence supplied by our dream
effect, but have been obtained by a direct analysis of what must,
logically, be the nature of any universe in which Time has length
and in which events are observed in succession' (p. 198 : emphasis his).

Since he himself thus insisted that Serialism was a trophy of
logical analysis, we may, with clear scientific consciences, at least
on this occasion, continue to neglect the—in any event—none too
impressive empirical material. I will now confront Dunne on his
own chosen ground of logical analysis. He was avowedly accepting
the suggestions of linguistic idiom :

'It is never entirely safe to laugh at the metaphysics of the "man-
in-the-street". Basic ideas which have become enshrined in popular
language cannot be wholly foolish or unwarranted. For that sort
of canonisation must mean, at least, that the notions in question
have stood the test of numerous centuries and have been accorded

unhesitating acceptance wherever speech has made its way . . .'
His idea was that temporal happenings involved *motion in a fourth
dimension*. Of course he did not *call* it a fourth dimension—his
vocabulary hardly admitted of that—but he was entirely convinced :

(1) That Time had length, divisible into "past" and "future".

(2) That this length was not extended in any Space that he
knew of. It stretched neither north-and-south, nor east-and-west,
nor up and down, but in a direction different from any of those
three—that is to say in a fourth direction.

(3) That neither the past nor the future was observable. All
observable phenomena lay in a field situated at a unique "instant"
in the Time length—an instant dividing the past from the future—
which instant he called "the present".

(4) That this "present" field of observation *moved* in some
queer fashion along the Time length, so that events which *were
at first* in the future *became* present and *then* past. The past was
constantly growing' (pp. 130 and 131 : italics and other punctua-
tion original).

Dunne continues : 'the employment of these references [i.e. the
words he has italicised—A.F.] to a sort of Time behind Time is
the legitimate consequence of having started with the hypothesis
of a *movement* through Time's length. For motion in Time must
be timeable. If the moving element is everywhere along the Time
length at once, it is not moving. But the Time which times that
movement is another Time. And the 'passage' of that Time must
be timeable by a third Time. And so on *ad infinitum*' (pp. 131–2 :
italics original).

Dunne comments : 'It is pretty certain that it was because he
["the man-in-the-street" that is, earlier described as "the original
discoverer of Time"—A.F.] had a vague glimpse of this endless
array of Times, one, so to say, embracing the other, that our discoverer abandoned further analysis' (p. 132).

I in my turn have three comments to make on this argument :
firstly, there is indeed a large class of idioms which do suggest this
sort of thing; secondly, if this suggestion is accepted then the
infinite regress indicated by Dunne does indeed develop; and,
thirdly, it is quite wrong to do what Dunne does. It is, that is to

say, quite wrong to develop these suggestions and then to attribute the resulting metaphysical construction to the man-in-the-street—thus casting a mantle of everyday sobriety over the shoulders of a logical extravaganza.

(a) The first comment is easy to support. Dunne himself mentions some of these suggestive idioms : 'when tomorrow comes', 'when I get to such and such an age', 'the years roll by', and 'the stages of life's journey'. It is easy to go on adding to this list almost indefinitely. We speak of the future coming to meet us all, of the march of time, of time the ever-rolling stream, and (particularly during elections) of Marching Forward Looking Steadfastly into the Future. Such idioms do suggest that we live in 'a universe in which Time has length and in which events are observed in succession' (p. 198). Indeed, if we had to describe the class of idioms to which we are referring, we could scarcely do so better than by picking upon this as their distinguishing characteristic. We are, we might say, speaking of those idioms in which we talk of the events which occur in succession in the same place or to the same person as if they were, not different and successive events, but different objects or different places which were observed or visited one after another.

In the examples so far given the suggestion is made by a moribund metaphor. We talk, for instance, of the march of time; a march which must of course be a march from event to event. And this piece of picturesque language thus gives rise to the idea that—to borrow a phrase from Sir Arthur Eddington—'Events do not happen : we merely come across them'. But sometimes the forms of language promote the same idea more subtly, more insidiously. The expression, 'That is past', has what has often been called a grammatical similarity to the expression, 'This is dark'. This grammatical similarity may mislead into the assumption that pastness and darkness are logically similar characteristics. Thus misled we might argue that, since anything which actually possesses some characteristic, some quality like darkness, must exist somewhere, the event which has this supposedly similar quality of pastness must also exist somewhere. Hence, since it is manifestly not here now, perhaps it is secreted in some mysterious limbo which we must have left behind us on our forward march from the past into the future. Thus the same analogy is suggested again, this time more indirectly.

Suppose someone believes, too generously, that it is impossible that anyone but a fool could ever be misled by such grammatical resemblances as that of 'This is past' to 'This is dark' or 'This is crinkled'. Then let him consult, in particular, that able and independent-minded Cambridge philosopher J. M. E. MacTaggart. For MacTaggart undoubtedly did generate paradoxes, which he took to be metaphysical discoveries, by doing just this; and MacTaggart was no fool. He construed the words 'past', 'present', and 'future', that is, as if they were quality words with a logic on all fours with that of 'dark' or 'red', or 'crinkled'.[6]

More generally such a sceptic, like so many others, needs to reflect that verbal habits are habits; and, hence, are as hard both to make—and still more to break—as any other habits. It is, for instance, virtually impossible immediately and systematically to break the old-established, dyslogistic associations of such a phrase as 'conspicuous waste'; and to employ it—as Thorstein Veblen said he intended to do—as a neutral term in detached sociological analysis.[7] It is, again, a difficult and perhaps time-consuming matter to complete the dissociations and associations made necessary by the recognition that some term is radically ambiguous. Because the word in sense one is (not merely similar to but) physically the same as the same word in sense two, its appearance in either sense tends to activate, not only those associations and dispositions which are appropriate to that sense, but also those which belong rather to the other.[8] It is, once more, for reasons of the same fundamental kind that the employment of unfamiliar terminology, which must as such lack the established associations of a more familiar and down-to-earth vocabulary, is bound to diminish understanding. We should indeed know, and be warned, that it is often for just this reason that various sorts of specialists and insiders, who happen to have something to hide from possibly critical outgroupers, are studious to employ jargon as their chosen instrument of obfuscation.[9]

(b) My second comment is that Dunne has seen that if the suggestions made or insinuated by these idioms are adopted, then a mysterious infinite regress develops: 'If Time passes or grows or accumulates or expends itself or does anything whatever except

stand rigid and changeless before a Time-fixed observer, there
must be another Time which times that second Time, and so on
in an apparent series to infinity' (p. 158). Events do not happen:
we merely come across them. Then someone asks: 'We come
across them one *after* another, I suppose?' So the event of coming
across event number one must itself occur before the event of
coming across event number two. And the event of coming across
the event of coming across event number one must again itself
occur before the event of coming across the event of coming
across event number two. And here we have that infinite regress
which generated Dunne's theory: 'The glaring regress in the
notion of time was a thing which had intrigued me since I
was a child of nine. (I had asked my nurse about it.)' pp.
4–5).

(*c*) My third comment is that it is quite wrong of Dunne first to
develop this infinite regress from the suggestions of idiom, and
then to claim the respectability of everyday familiarity for his
metaphysical construction. It is quite wrong, that is, to attribute
this philosophical construction to the man-in-the-street, whose
ideas, 'canonised' and 'enshrined in popular language . . . have
stood the test of numerous centuries and have been accorded
unhesitating acceptance wherever speech has made its way' (p.
130). Dunne himself in effect admits that this attribution is unwarranted. For he concedes that the plain man's vocabulary does
not permit him to talk of a 'fourth dimension' (p. 130). Also,
Dunne says, after 'a vague glimpse of this endless array of Times
[he] abandoned further analysis' (p. 132).

The plain fact behind this picturesque talk about the man-in-
the-street, is surely, that our language is saturated with suggestions
which could be developed into every sort of paradox and absurdity. These suggestions may take the form either of metaphor
or of grammatical analogy. They are not adopted by the adult
layman. For he has been conditioned not to press metaphors to
literal absurdity and not to develop grammatical analogies into
paradox. But sometimes they are adopted and pressed, either
by the child in his unschooled simplicity or by the metaphysician
in his trained subtlety. It is not a coincidence that the *Alice* books,

which contain a vast collection of such paradoxes and absurdities, were written by a brilliant logician for the delight of an intelligent child.

I V

So far I have tracked down Dunne's infinite regress of time dimensions to its sources in idiom. Perhaps it is also possible to detect similar sources for his self-contradictions—absolute time and the absolute observers conceived as the last terms of series which are infinite, and which therefore by definition can have no last terms. Such expressions as 'at infinity' or 'to infinity' have a grammatical similarity to expressions like 'at this point' or 'to Norwich'. This might suggest that 'infinity' like 'Norwich' referred to a place or position, albeit in the case of 'infinity' to a rather queer sort of place or position. Hence it might further suggest that it is logically quite in order to talk of the last point in an infinite series, at infinity. Such mistakes have been made. They are reminiscent of the gaffe of the possibly legendary Nazi propaganist who was misled by a British report of bombs dropped at random into the rash claim that German aircraft had pressed home attacks on Random. They are reminiscent too of that possible misconception of the logic of the word 'nobody' which Lewis Carroll exploited in *Alice Through the Looking Glass:*

'I see nobody on the road', said Alice.
'I only wish I had such eyes,' the King remarked in a fretful tone. 'To be able to see Nobody! And at that distance too! Why it is as much as I can do to see real people, by this light!'

But this last suggestion as to the possible source of one of Dunne's errors is a speculation. All the other suggestions have been confirmed in substance by his own confessions.

V

Although I have now executed my original programme of detecting the sources in linguistic idiom of one particular—and particularly absurd—absurd theory, Dunne has made a challenge which must not be entirely ignored : 'And we might suppose that

every philosopher who found himself face to face with this conspicuous, unrelenting vista of Times behind Times would proceed, without a moment's delay, to an exhaustive and systematic
examination . . .' (p. 158). Or, again, in another passage, a passage in which he curiously writes of an infinite regress as 'a
curious logical development', Dunne complains of 'the usual
philosophic method of dealing with any regress [which] is to
dismiss it with the utmost promptitude, as something full of contradictions and obscurities' (p. 4).

Complaint against the philosophers for neglecting this possible
time regress is scarcely just. Certainly since Dunne wrote there
have been many papers by English-speaking philosophers address-
ing themselves to both these and other perplexities about time.[10]
But long before Dunne there had been many famous and less
famous philosophers eager—in Samuel Alexander's phrase—'to
take time seriously'. F. H. Bradley as well as MacTaggart had
been driven, by just such perplexities as we have been reviewing,
to the desperate yet delightful expedient of proclaiming that 'Time
is Unreal', that it is 'mere appearance', or what have you.[11]

(a) I cannot hope to do more here than suggest four possible ways
of handling such perplexities. The first way is this desperate yet
rather dashing resort of such old-time, heroic metaphysicians as
Bradley and MacTaggart—the defiantly preposterous proclama-
tion of the unreality of time. This is, of course, open to the irresistible and relentless gibes of Professor G. E. Moore, the spokesman
within philosophy of the plain man's common sense.[12] It is absurd
to say that time is unreal when we know perfectly well that after
breakfast we shall deal with our correspondence, and that before
breakfast we cut ourselves while shaving. We just cannot hold that
time is unreal. For we do most assuredly know a great many
temporal facts, such as those already mentioned. And what could
an insistence upon the reality of time be, if it is not an emphasising
of the reality of temporal facts? Again, we cannot hold that the
whole notion of time is self-contradictory. For there are not merely
possible but actual situations to which temporal descriptions may
correctly be applied. And what could it be to say that an expression is self-contradictory if it is not at least partly to say that there
is no situation, whether actual or merely conceivable, to which
that expression would correctly be applied?

(*b*) The second way is that of the real plain man, as opposed to some philosopher acting the plain man. This second way is to shrug the shoulders and to dismiss the perplexities unexamined with a 'Well I know time is real because so-and-so occurred before so-and-so and tomorrow I shall do this and that and the other'. This way is to shirk, not to treat the problem. It possesses all and only the same merits—and the same demerits—as those two famous unphilosophical philosophical refutations of Dr Samuel Johnson : Berkeley's philosophical idealism was, it will be remembered, disposed of by kicking a stone, 'I refute it thus'; while as for philosophical questions about the freedom of the will, 'We know our will is free, and there's an end on't.'

(*c*) The third way is that of Dunne—to accept the infinite regress and any other paradoxes as suggestions, or even as demands, that we should erect an elaborate structure of theory. This way lies disaster, as this article has tried to show.

(*d*) The fourth way is to see that the paradoxes and absurdities may have been generated by misleading grammatical analogies and metaphors. They may be the punishments which fall on those who succumb to the tempting siren songs of idiom. It has already been shown how the apparent similarity of such expressions as 'at infinity' or 'Nobody came' to expressions like 'at Norwich' or 'somebody came' might mislead into mistakes about the logic of our language (or of any other language in which similar similarities occur). Someone might be misled, as Dunne himself apparently was misled, by the similarity of 'at infinity' to such expressions as 'at Norwich', into the mistake of thinking that as 'Norwich' is the name of a place in Norfolk, so 'infinity' too must refer to another but remoter position, or to some point in a series. Someone might be similarly misled—if only in Wonderland—by the similarity of 'Nobody came' to 'Somebody came', into the mistake of thinking that 'Nobody' refers to somebody, but a very queer and rather tenuous somebody. Certainly some people have been—and are— misled into construing 'the unknown' as the definite description of some identifiable entity. Hence, surely, the appeal of such Occultist posters as 'The Unknown, is it nearer?'.

It is mistakes such as these which have come to be called mistakes about the logic of our language. They consist in treating a word which is of one logical type as if it were a word of a different logical type. We are enticed into such errors by the grammatical similarities of words of one logical type to words of another logical type. We treat 'infinity' as if, like 'Norwich', it was the name of a place. The King treats 'Nobody' as if it referred to a mysterious 'Somebody'. In each case words of different logical types are treated as if they were logically similar. In each case we are misled by this irrelevancy of their grammatical similarity.

The fourth way of treating such paradoxes and absurdities as those to which Dunne drew attention is to exploit them as signs that some mistake has been made about the logic of our language. Taking this way we shall not, with Bradley and MacTaggart, think we have made a great ontological discovery, the discovery that Time is Unreal. Nor yet shall we, with Dunne, erect an edifice of theory upon foundations of paradox, under the misconception that we have discovered that time, so far from being unreal, is on the contrary far more complicated than had been thought; that there is, so to speak, both more to it and more of it than we had dared to suppose. Taking this fourth way we shall consider that the philosopher who, in generating a paradox, thinks he has made a discovery has probably made a mistake. Yet if he only realises that a mistake has been made, then he is halfway to making a discovery. For by detecting the sources of such paradoxes and absurdities in linguistic idiom, the philosopher can hope to make discoveries, not as once was hoped, about the ultimate and mysterious nature of reality, but discoveries less exciting about the structure and logic of the languages in which we talk and theorise about the universe around us.

VI

If this paper were being written only for people whose interests are primarily philosophical, it would have stopped already, at the end of Section V. But since it is in fact being written for a collection of articles likely to be seen by many whose concerns are primarily parapsychological, it may perhaps be modestly helpful to say a word about the employment of the term 'dimension'. For Dunne was by no means the only parapsychological theoretician to believe that the phenomena, or alleged phenomena, of parapsychology require us 'to introduce a new dimension' (p. 4);

though he perhaps was, even by the generous standards of parapsychological theorising, a shade extravagant in his further conviction that he was under a 'logical compulsion' to introduce not
merely one but an infinite series of new dimensions.

The continuing appeal of such ideas seems to lie in two areas.
In the first place the phenomena, or alleged phenomena, of parapsychology are just about as mind-boggling as mind-boggling can
be. It is indeed a more or less explicit defining characteristic of
a genuine parapsychological phenomenon that this should be so,
since such phenomena have to be unamenable to subsumption
under presently-established concepts and theories. Consequently,
the fact that what is offered as explanatory is itself excessively
difficult, if not impossible, to understand, is bound to seem, if
anything, a general point in its favour.

In the second place the particular suggestion of compassing the
explanation of radically recalcitrant phenomena by the postulation
of a further dimension, or further dimensions, is bound to appear
appropriate to children of our century. For we have all heard,
even if few of us have understood, talk of how certain ongoings,
which simply could not be fitted into the old—and as it had come
to seem—commonsensical Newtonian framework, can nevertheless
be comfortably squared with a new system of ideas, a system which
speaks of the universe as a 'four-dimensional space–time continuum'.

Clearly both these attractions have been felt both by members
of Dunne's by now enormous audience and by Dunne himself.
He himself seems to have posessed a greater than average knowledge of mathematics and physics; while their awareness of this
helped to increase the respect, if not the critical alertness, of his
readers. Now to say all this is not, of course, to say that anyone
was wrong to be attracted or impressed by the notion of postulating extra dimensions. Such an exercise in the speculative sociology
of knowledge can at most show why some people found, or find,
certain notions attractive. Yet to say that this or that notion is
attractive to the bourgeois, or to whites, or to the middle class, or
to any other group disfavoured by your true left-thinking sociolo-
gist, is not even to begin to show that the notion in question is
either erroneous or unfounded.

Reasons have, however, been given already, in previous sections of the present paper, for concluding that Dunne's Serialism is not so much erroneous or unfounded as simply incoherent. The two further and more general points which still need to be made refer to the significance to be attached to proposals to postulate further dimensions.

The first such more general point is that the expression 'to postulate an extra dimension' (of either time or space) is not one which already possesses determinate sense in today's ordinary nontechnical English. So if anyone is eager to equip it with such a sense, the onus must be upon him first to explain his proposal; and only thereafter to attempt to justify it. Until and unless some satisfactory explanation is thus provided by the protagonist of dimensional postulation, our own inability to understand precisely, or even vaguely, what is intended ought to be construed, not as an indication of our lamentable and admitted intellectual incapacity, but rather as evidence that we are not prepared either to deceive ourselves or to be deceived by pretentious yet empty talk.

The second such more general point is that the one exemplary case, in which some technical sense surely has been given to talk of postulating an extra dimension, is one in which the postulation imposes demands which neither Dunne nor any other parapsychological theoretician has ever been in sight of beginning to meet. This one exemplary case, which is the case which led to the now familiar talk of the universe as a four-dimensional space-time continuum, required that application be found for a geometrical calculus of four, as opposed to three, dimensions : 'to postulate a fourth dimension' was thus given the meaning 'to hypothesise that there is appropriate application for a four-dimensional geometry'; while 'an n–dimensional geometry' or 'an n–dimensional geometrical calculus' was implicitly defined as one concerned with the spatial—or, perhaps better, the logical—relations between points determined by n–co-ordinates—points, that is, which need n–co-ordinates in order to become determinate.

If this is right, and any nonmathematician and nonphysicist is bound to have some qualms about such esoteric matters; and if, furthermore, this is the model for the dimensional postulations so often proposed in parapsychology, and certainly no other model has to my knowledge been mentioned : then we must realise that we really have not got any discussably determinate theoretical suggestion, until and unless we have been given some indication as to which of the available calculi it is proposed to try to apply, and how, and to what. In particular, what is to be measured in order to produce the physical or psychological values of the various co-ordinates? Without any answers to these fundamental questions we do not have either a false or an incomplete theory. We have instead no theory at all.

REFERENCES AND NOTES

(1) This article retraverses some ground originally covered in (either or both) a paper published under the same title in the *Cambridge Journal* for 1951, and the second Appendix to A. G. N. Flew, *A New Approach to Psychical Research* (London, C. A. Watts, 1953).

(2) G. Ryle, *Proceedings of the Aristotelian Society*, 1931–2, p. 170. This paper has since been reprinted: first, in A. G. N. Flew (ed.), *Logic and Language*. First Series (Oxford, Blackwell, 1951); and, again, in G. Ryle, *Collected Papers*, vol. II (London, Hutchinson, 1971).

(3) I go on and on about the meaning in this sort of context of 'precognition' in two other articles: one on 'Broad and Supernormal Precognition', in P. A. Schilpp (ed.), *The Philosophy of C. D. Broad* (New York, Tudor, 1959), and the other on 'Precognition', in P. Edwards (ed.), *Encyclopedia of Philosophy* (New York and London, Macmillan and Free Press, and Collier-Macmillan, 1967). So I will not say anything about this important subject here.

(4) J. W. Dunne, *An Experiment with Time,* 3rd edn (London, Faber, 1934).

(5) *Proceedings of the Aristotelian Society*, supplementary vol. XVI (1937), p. 199.

(6) See, for instance, his deservedly famous article on 'The Unreality of Time' in *Mind*, 1908. For further examples from other areas see my Philosophy and Language' in A. G. N. Flew (ed.), *Essays in Conceptual Analysis* (London, Macmillan, 1956, pp. 5–6.

(7) T. Veblen, *The Theory of the Leisure Class* (London and New York, Macmillan, 1899), pp. 97 ff. Such failures to come to terms with the force of habit are peculiarly scandalous in those pretending to be scientists of man and society.

(8) Two true-life examples should prove salutary: both because of the importance of the distinctions involved; and because of the outstanding abilities and philosophical training of those lapsing. The first was provided by the late Professor C. S. Lewis, who had been trained as a philosopher before he proceeded to distinguish himself as a teacher of English Literature. Having been, during a famous Oxford confrontation, persuaded by Professor G. E. M. Anscombe of the crucial difference

between a, or the, reason (evidencing) and a, or the, reason (causing), Lewis forthwith proceeded to insist that where there is a reason why in one of these senses there could not also be, by the same token, a reason why in the other sense too. See Lewis' reply to Anscombe's article in *Socratic Digest* (Oxford, Blackwell, 1950), pp. 15–16.

The second offender shall here be charitably nameless. Suffice it to say that he is both a well-known secular philosopher and—as will emerge—a devout Radical of a now too common type. He had in my presence first accepted that it is only in different senses of the word 'democratic' that, for instance, the (hated, because capitalist) German Federal Republic and the (admired, because socialist) German Democratic Republic can both claim to be democratic. For the former the crux is obviously what the populace in fact want—and that the electorate can vote the scoundrels out. For the latter the crux was allowed to be that the government represents the true interests of its people—whether or not they in their ignorance and fallibility happen to recognise this. Having thus, whether rightly or wrongly, accepted that two senses of the word 'democracy' were involved, this very un-Benthamite philosophical Radical forthwith proceeded to the defence of the (admired, because socialist) Socialist Bloc; on the grounds that these countries had evolved their own different sort of democracy. But, of course, to assent to the statements that this is democratic in sense one, and that that is democratic in sense two, is not to warrant the conclusion that this and that are different varieties of one and the same species, democracy. On the contrary: so far as it goes it implies the opposite.

(9) See, for instance, George Orwell's splendid essay on 'Politics and the English Language', first printed in *Horizon,* April 1946, and reprinted in various collections since. But let us not indulge ourselves in any complacent un-Orwellian illusion that this, or any other, form of depravity is the peculiar prerogative of one single special kind of other people.

In particular, general complaints against politicians come especially ill from average citizens in more or less democratic states. For democratic politicians are tempted to become demagogues only and precisely to the extent that they believe that their electorates will respond to demagoguery. In a word: we would not get false election promises if none of us was eager to believe these, rather than to demand a sober programme realistically presented.

(10) See R. M. Gale (ed.), *The Philosophy of Time* (London, Macmillan, (1968). The papers by Professors J. N. Findlay and J. J. C. Smart are especially relevant.

(11) See, for instance, MacTaggart, loc sit., and Bradley's *Appearance and Reality* (London and New York, Sonnenschein and Macmillan, 1893), Ch. IV.

(12) See, for instance, his 'A Defence of Common Sense', first published in J. H. Muirhead (ed.), *Contemporary British Philosophy*, Second Series (London and New York, Allen & Unwin and Macmillan, 1925).

5

RELIGION AND PSYCHICAL RESEARCH

by

JONATHAN HARRISON

In this article I shall not consider whether any religious doctrine is true, nor whether paranormal phenomena do in fact occur. I shall simply consider the relations between religion and psychical research, or what the implications for religion would be, if paranormal phenomena did occur. For this purpose I shall assume to be true any testimony which would be regarded as establishing conclusively any fact which did not have the high antecedent improbability of paranormal phenomena.

Psychical research might have a bearing on religion in three ways. First of all, it might be that the occurrence of various paranormal phenomena would make more (or, perhaps, less) probable the doctrines of some particular religion. Secondly, though not giving positive support to any religious doctrines, it might remove some obstacles in the way of accepting them. (It could do this, for example, if the accepted theories or presuppositions of modern science, predominantly physics, place an obstacle in the way of believing religious teaching, and if psychical research shows that some or all of these doctrines are not true.) Thirdly, psychical research might supply us with concepts which can be made use of in understanding religious phenomena and doctrines.

PSYCHICAL RESEARCH AND THE MAIN ARGUMENTS FOR THE EXISTENCE OF GOD

The only one of the three best-known arguments for the existence

G

of God which could be affected by the findings of psychical research would be the argument from design. The ontological argument could not be affected, since it has no existential premise for these findings to modify. The cosmological argument could not be affected, because it starts simply from the premise that something or other exists or occurs, the truth of which psychical research could scarcely throw doubt on. I can see no way, however, in which the argument from design is made any stronger or weaker by the findings of psychical research. Paranormal phenomena seem to exhibit just as much, or just as little, design as any of the more well attested phenomena of nature.

TELEKINESIS

Prima facie the occurrence of telekinesis would seem to make it more likely that miracles actually do occur. A large number of miracles appear to consist in some privileged person exercising control over some physical occurrence, usually outside his body, without producing this occurrence in any of the usual ways. For example, Christ changed water into wine, which was outside his body, without expanding or contracting his muscles, moving his limbs, finding grape concentrate and adding it to the water. Telekinesis consists in just this control, by the 'agent', of things (usually, though not necessarily, outside the confines of his body) without his first manipulating his muscles in any usual way.

One might wish to say that there is nothing so very extraordinary about telekinesis. All that happens, when I will a dice to turn up six, and, as a result, it does, is simply that something happens *outside* my body similar to something which is a normal occurrence inside my body. The case for this is as follows. When I try to raise my arm and succeed, either my trying to raise it causes it to rise, or it does not. If it does cause it to rise, the firing of neurons in my brain is affected by my trying to move my arm, and its rising cannot be completely explained by physiological happenings in my body. In other words, my trying to move my arms interferes with the firing of neurons inside my body. If it does not alter the firing of these neurons, then my trying to move my arm would make no difference to whether my arm rose or not, and I am not really responsible for any of my bodily movements.

Attempts have been made, of course, to show that my trying to move my arm and succeeding does not involve any mentally caused interruption to physiological processes occurring in my body, for example by trying to show that my trying to move my arm is just one physiological occurrence among others. I personally do not think any attempts so far made have been successful. If such an attempt were successful, perhaps the same technique could be used to show that my trying to change the water into wine or make a die turn up six, and succeeding, were just another physiological event. In this case, if I were ever to succeed in doing such things there would have to be action at a distance between a physiological event inside my head and a physical event somewhere else.

Though many of the difficulties involved in telekinesis are the same as those involved in the occurrence of miracles, telekinesis is not just a species of miracle. An event is a miracle not simply because the agent produces some effect outside his muscular control without first contracting or expanding his muscles in such a way as to initiate a causal chain resulting in the miraculous event. To be a miracle, an event must have the purpose of serving as a sign that some religious doctrine is true, and also, perhaps, be 'directly' produced by divine agency, involving an intervention in the normal course of nature. The word 'miracle', too, as well as the word 'telepathy', is in part honorific. If water is changed into wine in an extraordinary way, and for no good reason, it would not be a miracle, though teetotallers might wrongly suppose it to be one.

Unfortunately, if telekinesis were a fact, though this would make it more likely that various alleged extraordinary events actually occurred, it would make it less likely that they were miracles. If being a miracle implies some interruption to a natural law, then telekinesis, if it occurs, shows that it is not a law of nature that it is impossible for human beings to exercise direct control over events without first using their muscles to move their bodies or some part of their bodies. Hence various allegedly miraculous events are no interruption to this law of nature. Indeed, one would hope and expect that telekinetic phenomena, if they occur, are just as much law-governed as any other phenomena. In this case, we ought to be able to make use of the laws governing telekinetic phenomena in the way in which we make use of the laws of physics and chemistry to grow cabbages and bake cakes. The former operations would be no more miraculous than the latter.

On the other hand, if an event can be both miraculous and naturally explicable, as some theologians and philosophers have alleged, it really does not seem to matter very much whether telekinesis occurs or not. The putative miracles might then be explained by the normal laws of nature.

It might be argued that the study of telekinesis gives us a concept which helps us understand the manner in which God exercises control over events which occur in the universe. I doubt very much, however, whether it does any such thing. The reason why it might be supposed to supply us with such a concept is this. Since God is omnipotent, he must be able to prevent anything that occurs. If he were to do this, however, he could not do it in any way analogous to the way in which men prevent things from occurring, for men to do this by moving their muscles in certain appropriate ways, and God does not have any muscles, or a body in any straightforward sense. We might then wish to argue that He affects the course of nature in the way in which men with telekinetic powers affect the course of nature, for example by willing certain things to occur which consequently occur. God's activity, however, can bear little resemblance to telekinetic intervention by men. Man's willing an event to occur is itself an event, which takes place at a certain time, and is either simultaneous with or slightly later than the event he wills. God cannot will things in this way, however, unless he performs actions which take place in time. God, however, is generally conceived of as being outside time.

The other alleged religious phenomenon upon which telekinesis might be supposed to have some bearing is the efficacy of petitionary prayer. If petitionary prayer is effective, something must happen which one has prayed for and, furthermore, it must happen because one has prayed for it.

It is quite obvious, of course, that petitionary prayer may have effects, and sometimes desirable effects, on the person doing the praying. These effects may be divided into two kinds. Firstly, there are side-effects, in other words effects on the person doing the praying, other than the accomplishment of that for which he is praying. If someone were to pray for the health of someone near to him, feel better as a result of praying, and so work more effectively, this would be a side-effect of his praying. Secondly, someone may pray that something shall happen to him with the effect that this thing does happen to him. For example, he may pray that he shall be less anxious, and, as a result, become less anxious. Neither of these can count as the answering of a prayer. The first does not count, because what happens to the man who prays is not what he prayed for. The second does not count because, though what happened to the man who prays is what he prayed for, and though it would not have happened to him unless he had prayed for it, his getting what he prayed for is perfectly understandable in terms of the ordinary laws of nature. It fully accords with what we know about human psychology that some- one who believes that there is a God who will help him with his burdens will be relieved of anxiety if he prays for such relief.

Hence, if prayers are to count as being answered, there must not be a normal connection of cause and effect between our pray- ing and our getting what we pray for. But for the same reason, there must not be a paranormal connection either. For if our get- ting what we pray for is the natural, though paranormal, result of our praying, then our prayer is not granted. It is granted only if God intervenes in the normal course of events on our behalf. Hence if psychical research showed that praying could normally affect the behaviour of inanimate objects in a paranormal way, this would tend to show that prayers were not granted, but simply had consequences which more orthodox studies would not lead us to expect.

TELEPATHY

It is an assumption both of common sense and of normal science that an event in the mind of one person cannot affect any event in the mind of another, except indirectly. The one event must affect the body of the person whose mind this mind is, these effects must be transmitted, by means of waves, particles or phy- sical contact, to the body of the second person, and these effects in their turn must modify what is going on in his mind. For example, I feel hungry and wish my hunger to be assuaged. This causes me to move my jaws, lips and vocal chords in such a way as to produce the words 'I feel hungry'. This in turn causes sound waves to pass through the air, fall on the ear-drums of my friend Smith, which transmits nervous impulses to Smith's brain. These cause him to have the thought that I feel hungry, and, if I am lucky, to give me food.

If telepathy occurs, there is direct causal connection between something going on in one person's mind and something going on in another person's mind, which is not brought about by means of this physical link between their bodies.

The normal kind of telepathy occurs when one person looks at a card and another person is asked to guess the card that he is looking at. Telepathy is supposed to occur if he does this successfully, significantly more often than could be due to chance, in circumstances when no ordinary physical transmission can be taking place between the body of the one person and the body of the other. In the cases usually discussed, the effect on the 'receiver' is cognitive; it consists in his knowing or believing that something is the case. Sometimes, however, this cognitive effect is derivative from some other effect. For example, the effect of telepathy on the receiver may be, in the first instance, to cause him to have the mental image of an aspidistra, from which he may conclude that the 'sender' is seeing an aspidistra. In all these cognitive cases there has to be a causal connection between what is going on in the mind of the sender and in the mind of the receiver. If there were no such connection, it would be pure coincidence that the receiver believes what he does, and so such beliefs could not amount to knowledge.

There is no logical reason why this direct causal connection between one mind and another should be confined to cases where the effect of what is going on in the sender's mind is to produce knowledge in the receiver of what is going on in the mind of the former. It might be to produce some piece of knowledge other than this. For example, the sender's knowledge of the whereabouts of a will might cause the receiver to come to know the whereabouts of this will. Such effects might be even more various. It might be that sometimes my feelings and decisions were the direct result of what was going on in someone else's mind. If so, such effects would be extremely difficult to detect. In those special cases when the effect on the receiver is to cause him to believe something about the sender, this belief stands out from the other contents of his mind, in that it *presents* itself to him as a belief about the contents of someone else's mind apparently not acquired in a normal way. If my feelings were directly affected by what was going on in someone else's mind, the feelings which were so affected would be just like the feelings which were not, and so there would be no reason why we should look for a paranormal explanation of the former's occurrence. It *could* be that our feelings, decisions and beliefs (other than those presenting themselves as paranormally acquired) were being affected by what was going on in other people's minds all the time, without our even so much as suspecting it.

I doubt whether the study of telepathy could show that there is direct non-inferential awareness of the contents of others' minds, analogous to direct non-inferential awareness of the contents of one's own mind. Sometimes what is alleged to happen is something like this. Smith actually sees a tulip, or is asked to visualise one. Jones, in another room, or perhaps in another town, is asked what Smith is seeing or visualising, and replies 'Smith is visualising a tulip.' Sometimes he does this because the image of a tulip appears in his own mind, and he infers from this that Smith is seeing a tulip. Jones is not directly aware of Smith's seeing or visualising the tulip, nor is there any reason to suppose that the mental image of a tulip before Jones' mind is numerically identical with the mental image of a tulip before Smith's mind. Their images are seldom, if ever, precisely similar, and, even if they were, it would not follow that they were identical. Indeed, what the criteria for saying that they were identical are, are not clear. Sometimes Smith may have an unfounded belief, not accompanied by a mental image, that Smith is seeing or visualising a tulip. I cannot make up my mind whether such beliefs would amount to knowledge, even if they were correct in a high proportion of cases, and there were reason to suppose that the receiver's belief about the sender's mental state would not exist unless the sender's were in that state. An unfounded true belief about someone else's mind which is in fact caused by that which it is about, even if it amounts to knowledge, is not the same thing as a direct awareness of what is going on in someone else's mind. If someone knows

from past experience that he has such true beliefs in a high proportion of cases, then he is justified in inferring things about the contents of other people's minds from the occurrence of his beliefs.
His knowledge then rests upon an argument of the form : Whenever I have an unfounded belief about the contents of someone
else's mind, this belief turns out to be true; I have an unfounded
belief to the effect that Smith is in distress; therefore Smith is in
distress. Such an argument would be a perfectly ordinary case of
induction by simple enumeration, and in no way eccentric. Its
major premise, that my unfounded beliefs about other people's
minds are true, would have to be established by finding out in
normal ways what the contents of these minds were.

If petitionary prayer sometimes affects the behaviour of other
people, it would presumably do this by modifying their beliefs or
wants in a 'paranormal' way. Hence if telepathy were known to
occur, it would make it more rational and less irrational to believe
that other people's behaviour was sometimes affected by prayers
in some way other than the usual ways, for example by their dis-
covering that it was what we were praying for and getting or
helping to get it for us. But, as I have said, getting what you
pray for, even if it is the case that you would not have got what
you prayed for if you had not prayed for it, does not mean that
prayers are granted. For prayers to be granted, there must be a
God, who gives us what we pray for, and who would not have
given us what we prayed for, if we had not prayed for it. If telepathy were a fact, this would suggest that we might get what we
prayed for in paranormal ways, even if there is not a God to give
us what we pray for. If there are laws governing whether we get
what we pray for, then it looks as if praying for people to behave
in certain ways is, so to speak, a self-sufficient way of affecting
others' behaviour. It is just because we think that there is no law
to the effect that praying for someone to do something may cause
him to do that thing that we feel we need to postulate that there is
a God who interferes with the normal course of nature on our behalf.
If there is such a law, there is no need to explain the production
of such effects by divine intervention, any more than there is any
need to explain by divine intervention why water boils if it is
heated. The effect of assimilating getting what you pray for to a
wider class of phenomena, in which what goes on in one person's

mind is affected by what goes on in another person's mind, would be to suggest that the fact that it was *praying* that modified others' behaviour was not the essential thing about it. For if there are ways of modifying others' behaviour paranormally which do not consist in praying that they should be modified, what prayer and these may have in common cannot be that what is essential to prayer, namely, that it consists in a request to a supposed supreme being that he intervene in some way on our behalf, is what makes it effective. That it is *prayer* which modifies others' behaviour would therefore be coincidental and inessential.

God is supposed to know our inmost thoughts, and this without being told, or having to infer them from our words, facial expressions and behaviour. The possibility of his knowing our thoughts in this way presents considerable conceptual difficulties.

The concept of God's inferring what our thoughts are, or inferring anything else for that matter, is itself a difficult one. For (a) inference involves a passage from something one knows to something one does not, which is impossible in the case of a being who is omniscient, and (b) occurs at a given date, which is impossible in the case of a being to whom temporal predicates do not apply. On the other hand, God's knowing without inference our thought and feelings is itself not free from difficulty, for it is sometimes alleged that any thought or feeling which I know of without inference is by definition mine; hence my feelings will be both God's and mine.

If I am right, however, in suggesting that telepathy does not involve any direct awareness by one person of the thoughts of another, telepathy provides us with no help in solving the problem of how God knows our thoughts. The idea of God inferring, from the fact that images of naked women spring to his mind, that I am so wicked as to be imagining naked women, is ridiculous. So is the idea that unfounded beliefs about my thoughts, which he has learnt by past experience to rely on, spring into his mind.

What is known as the argument from religious experience is not, strictly speaking, an *argument* for the existence of God. It consists in maintaining that, because we have some direct knowledge of God, we have some way of knowing that he exists which does not involve having recourse to argument. We know that material objects exist because we perceive them, not because we infer from certain premises that there must be such things. Similarly, it is said, we know that God exists because we do something like perceive him, and do not argue to his existence from doubtful premises such as that the universe exhibits signs of having been designed.

However, where perception of material objects is concerned, light waves emanate from the object perceived and impinge upon our eyes, sound waves upon our ears, or part of the surface of our body is in physical contact with part of the surface of the object perceived; these things, then, cause nervous impulses to pass from our nerve endings to our brain. In any direct awareness of the existence of God, if such there be, nothing analogous can be involved. For God does not have a body, with which we might be in physical contact, or from which light or sound waves might emanate. Hence any direct knowledge we possess of God or his existence must be somewhat analogous to telepathic knowledge. We must have mental images of perceptions which, properly interpreted, give us knowledge about his existence and nature, or the fact that he wants us to do certain things; alternatively the belief that he has these wants must spring to our mind, and cause us to conclude that he does in fact want us to do those things.

In the case of telepathic knowledge of the minds of other human beings, we can check by normal means on what we think we know telepathically. If we think that we have telepathic knowledge that Smith is looking at flowered wallpaper, or is in distress, we can confirm or disconfirm our belief simply by asking him. If we think we may have telepathic knowledge of God's mind, however, there is no normal way of checking our belief.

PRECOGNITION

Normally all our knowledge of the future is obtained by inference involving a major premise of the form 'Whenever such-and-such, then so-and-so later.' If precognition occurs, we have certain apparently unfounded beliefs about the future which turn out to be true more frequently than can be put down to coincidence, or dream or waking imagery which can be interpreted as giving information about what is going to happen.

I can personally see little religious significance in the occurrence of precognition. God's foreknowledge cannot be understood as being similar to it. He could scarcely be expected to infer things about the future from his imagery, or to have unexplained hunches, which turn out to be true, about what was going to happen. In any case, God would not need precognition, as he would have ample knowledge of what had happened in our past and present, and the laws which connect this with what is going to happen in our future.

There are stories in the Bible, some of which are about Christ, of various apparent precognitive occurrences. If precognition is known to occur, this should make us more ready to believe such stories. On the other hand, to the extent that Christ is supposed to be uniquely endowed with such paranormal powers, the everyday occurrence of precognition, though it makes more likely that he has these powers, makes it less likely that they are supernatural, or that he was unique in possessing them. He might, however have been unique in the *degree* in which he possessed them.

If God is outside the sequence of temporally ordered events, his knowledge of what we think of as future cannot, strictly speaking, be called *pre*cognitive. Perhaps God, from his atemporal vantage point, sees the whole of life history of the universe in one timeless and dateless act. In this case, a study of precognition will have even less bearing upon his knowledge of our future than I have suggested.

CLAIRVOYANCE

Clairvoyance seems to me to have little relevance to religion. Claims to clairvoyance are made on behalf of Christ, and if the existence of clairvoyance is established, this would make it more likely that such claims are true. On the other hand, it would weaken the claim that Christ was unique, to the extent that this claim is based on his being unique in possessing such powers. It might, however, be that he possessed such powers to a unique degree.

God's knowledge of the physical order must be clairvoyant, since God does not possess a body, and so does not possess sense organs.

APPARITIONS

Our concept of a normal, fully-fledged material object is the concept of something with a front, back and inside, standing in spatial relations to other material objects, perceptible by all normal observers from different points of view and to more than one sense, having mass, and affecting other material objects, and so on. It is possible to find or conceive things which fall short of this standard in various ways. Rainbows are not tangible and only visible from a limited range of points of view. Mirror images have fronts, but not backs. Liver spots are only visible, and to one person at that, and it is impossible to weigh them or look at them from the back. Hallucinations are usually private, often involve one sense only, are of comparatively short duration, and do not obey the laws of physics, though sometimes they seem to. (Hallucinations sometimes throw hallucinatory shadows.)

Apparitions, if they occur, belong to that class of phenomena which divagate from the fully-fledged material objects in various different ways. Often they are not perceptible to everybody. Often, too, they are not perceptible to more than one sense. Though they seem to behave fairly naturally for the most part, they do not leave physical traces, and so cannot be photographed, and may disappear through walls or closed doors. Apparitions thus closely resemble hallucinations, but are unlike hallucinations in that the latter are 'purely subjective', in other words, they are productions entirely of the mental and physical state of the person who has them. Apparitions, however, are 'objective', or involve receptiveness to something outside the person who perceives them, to the extent that they frequent a given locality, or are causally dependent upon the occurrence of some emergency in the life of a relative or close friend.

The most obvious application of any positive findings of psychical research to religion would lie in the suggestion that the Christ who appeared after his crucifixion was in fact a post mortem apparition, a possibility which the accounts of these appearances do in a variety of ways suggest. (This would dissolve my childish puzzle, about why Christ's clothes, as well as his body, were resurrected. This would then become a phenomenon similar to the fact that hallucinatory limbs block from view, or are themselves hidden by, real objects). If so, then, to the extent that the belief that *our* bodies will one day be resurrected gains support from the fact that Christ's body was resurrected, (and we believe that Christ's body was resurrected in part because we believe he needed it to make the appearances he did after his crucifixion), this belief is completely undermined if what the disciples saw after the crucifixion was not a physical body of any kind, but an apparition. Furthermore, if the Christ the disciples saw after the crucifixion was an apparition, it is not essential even that Christ's *mind* survived his bodily death, for it is usually, though perhaps not always, unnecessary to postulate a mind standing to apparitions in a relation similar to that in which our bodies stand to our minds. Most apparitions no more have minds than do hallucinations or pictures of people on a television screen; indeed, many apparitions are supposed to be of people who are not yet dead, and whose minds are quite normally inhabiting their own bodies. (The word 'apparition' may be a bad one, in that it is too much like the word 'ghost', with its popular association with a translucent stuff which is inhabited by the mind of some person deceased. For this reason it may sometimes be better to talk of quasi-hallucinations.[1] Quasi-hallucinations differ from ordinary hallucinations in that they are paranormally induced and that they give some objective information about the world, such as that a near relative, whom the quasi-hallucination resembles, has recently died.)

Among the stories in religious literature there are many about those who have received communications in visual or auditory form allegedly from God or from those of lesser rank in the divine hierarchy. *Prima facie,* it is rather important that these visual or auditory experiences should not be entirely hallucinatory, for, if so, they are entirely the product of the physical and mental state of the person having them, and can reveal nothing except facts about him. The concept of an apparition may be capable of dealing with some of these phenomena. What is needed is the concept of a visual or auditory phenomenon which simulates the appearance of ordinary material objects, including people's bodies, or the noises which emanate from them, but which nevertheless, is not a mere hallucination, but revelatory of some objective feature of reality. Joan of Arc's voices, presumably, were not caused by sound waves impinging on her ear drums. Nevertheless, if they are to be regarded as veridical religious phenomena, she must have obtained from them information which was true, or advice which was sensible, or commands which ought to be obeyed, but which were beyond her own resources. Hence her 'hallucinations' or 'apparitions' must have enabled her to come into contact with a divine source and extend her knowledge by this means.

Would the occurrence of apparitions strengthen or weaken the belief in divine communication by means of quasi-hallucinatory visual or auditory experiences? In one way it would strengthen this belief, for, if apparitions occur, it would be impossible to reject the latter views out of hand, on the ground that they involved an extension of the percipient's perceptual knowledge which did not involve any action upon his sense organs. In another way, however, they might weaken the belief, for it opens the possibility that such occurrences really belong together with a mass of secular phenomena, and have been misconstrued in a religious way by people whose beliefs predisposed them to favour such an interpretation. (The same, of course, would be true if they were in fact simply hallucinations.) Joan of Arc's voices might have given her good advice, which was beyond her own resources, but which, nevertheless, was the paranormal product of someone else's mind, or of her own subliminal mind.

APPARITIONS AND LIFE AFTER DEATH

I would be naïve to suppose that at some future date the natural order will be suddenly suspended, the bones of the dead arise from their graves, be reclothed with flesh, and reassume the mental powers and characteristic dispositions of their former owners. If we do not conceive of resurrection like this, however, how are we to conceive of it? In particular, where are we to find room for the resurrected bodies, for heaven, and for hell?

One way would be to conceive of heaven and hell, and the bodies of their inhabitants, as inhabiting a separate space, or spaces, objects in which stand in no spatial relations to things in the world in which we at present find ourselves. Such objects could not be reached from any point in this world, for however long we travelled. This would, I think, be a logically possible but not very plausible, hypothesis.

An alternative possibility would be to conceive of resurrected bodies as being something like apparitions. These have the advantage of not being visible to everybody, which could explain why we cannot see people in heaven or hell. Since apparitions do not exclude material objects from the space they appear to occupy, there would be no difficulty about finding room for them in the space of ordinary material objects.

The most satisfactory model for the after-life would seem to be suggested by the following phenomenon. An apparition of a person is seen, and possibly heard, at a certain place, and at the same time this person himself has clairvoyant or out-of-the-body experiences of seeing, and possibly also hearing, from this very place. This suggests the possibility of a community of people with apparition bodies communicating by auditory apparition words, or apparition gestures. Such a fantasy, however, would differ from the cases that have actually been reported. When this happens to Tom and Dick, one of them perceives the body of the other *in* a place where it is not, and the other perceives the body of the first *from* a place where his body is not. If they were in the next world, Tom and Dick would be embodied in apparitions only. I see no very good reason why a person should not have only an apparition body.[2] A very determined identity theorist might even say that, though the thoughts of normal people were just brain processes, the thoughts of people in heaven or in hell were apparition processes.

Though the study of apparitions may give us a concept which enables us to understand talk about heaven and hell, the study of apparitions does little to make it any more likely that there are such places. Apparitions, however, have been reported which appear to transmit communications from some deceased person.

The model for heaven and hell which I have suggested makes possible some rapprochement between those who believe in the resurrection of the body and those who believe in the immortality of the soul. It is to some extent a matter of arbitrary choice whether you describe those in the next world, if it is as I have suggested, as having a body or as not having a body. They would not have a body in that they would not be embodied in any material stuff, obeying the laws of physics and chemistry. On the other hand they would not *not* have a body, in that they would be engaged solely in pure thought, but also feel and perceive (albeit in a way that is quasi-hallucinatory). Hence they would have perceptions and feelings *as* of having bodies themselves, and perception as of the bodies of others.

If you accept a phenomalist account of ordinary material objects, the difference between a real body and an apparition body becomes something like one of degree. Statements about real bodies are then statements about the perceptions of observers, and so are statements about apparition bodies. The difference would lie largely in the fact that we cannot obtain perceptions of apparition bodies, but others, in the next world, can, and in that perceptions of bones and brain cells of bodies in this world are obtainable, but perceptions of bones and brain cells of apparition bodies are not obtainable.

OUT-OF-THE-BODY EXPERIENCES

Though the occurrence of out-of-the-body experiences would strengthen the hand of those who believe that disembodied existence is logically possible, they do not provide much reason for thinking that it actually occurs. Out-of-the-body experiences happen to people who in fact have bodies, and so it may well be that they would not, or even could not, have had out-of-the-body experiences if they had not had bodies.

If out-of-the-body experiences ever give those who have them knowledge of the events they seem to witness from places in space outside their bodies, this weakens the claim that we are so tied to our bodies that veridical preception is impossible without a suitable modification to our sense organs. It also strengthens the claim that such people actually were, in some sense or other, situated in a place outside their bodies, for this is the place from which they perceive.

REINCARNATION

It is a Hindu belief that everyone, when he dies, is reincarnated in the body of some other human being or animal, and that everyone was incarnated in a similar way before he was born. Some evidence has been brought to light that some people are reincarnations of former people. For example, a child with parents A and B, living in a village X, seems ill at ease in his own environment, but at home with parents C and D (who have recently lost a child) in village Z. He regards C and D as his parents, and Z as his village, and has memories of C and D and Z which he cannot have obtained by normal means. There is therefore some reason for treating A and B's child as a reincarnation of C and D's child.

This, however, is not the only way of dealing with this situation. One might say that A and B's child was not the same person as C and D's child, but simply seemed to remember seeing and doing some of the things C and D's child actually saw and did. In any case, such cases would appear to be at most occasional freaks. There is no evidence that everyone is reincarnated. Indeed, what could be the cash value of such a claim, or what could it amount to, if there were no ways at all in which a person could be caused to remember those things he is alleged to have done in some former incarnation?

MEDIUMSHIP AND LIFE AFTER DEATH

There are a variety of paranormal phenomena which ostensibly involve communication with us by 'people' who have died. Messages may be spelt out by a Ouija or planchette board, by the hands of some person not attending to what he is doing, or by the lips of a medium, and these messages apparently come from some deceased person. (This deceased person either speaks to us directly with the medium's vocal apparatus, or more, frequently, passes on messages to a 'control', who is almost certainly a subsidiary personality of the medium herself.) These phenomena raise fascinating problems, but here is not the place to go into them. The question before us is not whether these things happen, or what interpretation is to be put upon them, but whether they have any bearing upon religion. For us, the most important bearing they could have would be to establish the truth of the Christian belief that, after an interval, we are resurrected with some kind of body, and then find ourselves, according to the strength of our faith or the extent of our works, in heaven or in hell. (It is scarcely necessary

H

to point out that the two beliefs, that there is a God, and that there is life after death, are logically independent of one another. One might be true without the other, or they might both be false.)

It seems to me that, if we accept them at their face value, these communications, ostensibly from those who have died, do nothing whatsoever to establish a belief in an afterlife in heaven or in hell. Resurrection is something that is supposed to happen to everybody, whereas there is good evidence only of survival happening to a very small minority. Indeed, it is possible that those who survive do not experience one, or even two, common unitary worlds at all. It is even possible that survival is something purely temporary and sporadic, which happens only during the period of the medium's trance and neither before nor after. Resurrection is supposed to be either markedly pleasant, or markedly unpleasant, whereas, according to the evidence, the state of those who communicate with us is often not markedly pleasant, and, though frequently not such as a discerning person would wish to find himself in, seldom markedly unpleasant either. So far as is known, there is no correlation between one's faith or works in this world and one's state in the world or worlds revealed to us by these communications. Nor are there any known ways of ensuring either that one will survive, or that one will not survive, or ensuring that, if one does survive, one's state is pleasant rather than otherwise. There is, indeed, little to suggest that survival of death is not simply an unfortunate accident which happens to some people. It may be that the obscurity of most of the messages is due to the difficulty of sending them, but there is, I suppose, the dreadful possibility that the trauma of death has a shattering effect on those who suffer it and survive. (I, personally, would rather not survive than run the risks of what might happen to me if I did.) It could be, of course, that as well as this twilight world to which the empirical facts point there is also a Christian resurrection, but such an arrangement would seem a little uneconomical.

One might also expect the phenomena exhibited by trance mediumship to throw some light on the phenomenon of (apparent) possession. For sometimes mediums or the bodies of mediums appear to be possessed by the minds of those who have died, and make their movements, and speak with their voice. Of course, psychiatric illness is also likely to throw light on such phenomena, but when we describe something as an illness there is, embedded in what we say, a value judgement. If someone behaves as if possessed, and much worse than he usually does, we say, he is ill, but if he behaves as if possessed, and better than he usually does, we are inclined to say that he is inspired. Just as a medium may say words without herself being conscious of saying them, so, when we are inspired, we write words, or compose music, or paint pictures or solve problems which we ourselves have not consciously rehearsed or excogitated or envisaged or puzzled over. Of course one says, for what it is worth, that it is done unconsciously, but in this assertion the operative expressions seems to be 'it is done'; it would be going a bit too far, be too arrogant, or not quite accurate, to say we did it. Indeed, if paranormal phenomena show anything, they join with certain phenomena of abnormal psychology, for example hysterical dissociation, to suggest that the borders between one mind and another may not be as clear as one might be inclined to suppose. Were there, for example, four minds associated with Miss Beauchamp's one body, or was there one mind, dissociated into four subsidiary bits? When the solution to a problem presents itself to us without our consciously having thought about it, was it one mind (our own) which solved the problem, albeit unconsciously, or was there a mind which solved the problem, and another mind to which this solution was passed on? One might wish to say that there *must* be one mind only, because I obtain the solution without its having reached me by way of any of my normal senses. All this shows, however, is that what problem solving there was was useful to me, and had effects on me which did not come about by means of contact with my bodily senses. If telepathy occurs—and, perhaps, even if it is conceivable—we should shrink from saying that a mental process is mine simply because it has direct effects on mental processes which unequivocally are mine, for in that case some mental processes would have to belong to two people (though one should not jump too quickly to the conclusion that even this is impossible). For a process which one person is conscious of could then have direct effects on the mind of another person. In these cases the thinking, which one may have to postulate in order to explain the finished product, if it is not mine, is not that of any *other* normal person. In the phenomena of trance mediumship, however, the mental forces which affect the medium, which are *prima facie* not hers, may be someone else's, in other words, belong to someone who is now dead.

All this is not wholly unlike the religious phenomenon of gaining strength and help, guidance and inspiration from an ostensibly supernatural source. What is sometimes put down to God's grace may in fact be due to the operation of subliminal or unconscious activity which is of a similar nature. I am doubtful, however, to what extent they strengthen the religious hypothesis that this source is divine. They tend to strengthen the belief that the help comes from outside ourselves, but to weaken the belief that it is a *supernatural* source outside ourselves. Nor are such phenomena exclusively religious. The experience of being inspired from outside is certainly not confined to religious people. It does not necessarily present itself in a religious manner, nor is it necessarily a good thing that it occurs. Sometimes, doubtless, it is indifferent, and at other times positively evil. And though religious devotees may be familiar with techniques for releasing or harnessing such 'extra personal' forces, and they themselves ask for and think they are getting divine guidance, I am not at all sure that the success of these techniques in practice shows that the beliefs of those who practise these techniques are correct. You may ask for divine guidance, and get guidance and inspiration, but this does not show that your belief that you have been divinely guided is a true one.

PSYCHICAL RESEARCH AND CHRISTOLOGY

It is, of course, an orthodox Christian belief that Christ was God. This is something which many people, myself included, find very difficult to accept. For one thing, God is supposed to have many attributes which Christ did not have, and *vice versa*. God is omnipotent, but Christ was not; Christ could walk, but God cannot. It is, however, a commonplace that those who say that Christ was God are simply putting in a paradoxical way some truth which they find very difficult to express satisfactorily otherwise. But what could this truth be? It may be that the mind of Christ stood in some especially intimate relation to the mind of God. God, because he is omniscient, must have known everything about Christ's thoughts, feelings and volitions, presumably without inferring them. Christ must, if the stories in the gospels and what he himself said are both true, have known a great deal about God's mind without inference. Furthermore, there is not the usual reason, in the case of God and Christ—namely, that they are associated with different bodies—for wishing to draw a clear-cut distinction between God's mind and Christ's; though Christ had a body, God does not, or not in any straightforward sense. If we also assume that there was a direct nonphysical causal connection between God's mind and Christ's (which there might have to be, since God does not have a body), and that one reason for wanting to say that a mental process of which we are not conscious is our own unconscious mental process, is that it has a direct effect on our own conscious mental processes, then there is perhaps some reason for thinking that the borderline between Christ's mind and God's was not clearly delineated. Hence there may be some reason for thinking that the question, 'Were there two minds, or one?' is not a clear question. It may follow from this that the question, 'Were there two persons, or only one?' is also not a clear question.

This suggestion has the difficulty that it must apply to everyone, not simply to Christ, in some degree, since God knows without inference the mental processes of everybody, and can never causally affect these mental processes *via* the manipulation of their owner's body when their owner has not got one.

POLTERGEISTS

If there are poltergeists, material objects move about in a way which the existence of antecedent forces, like winds and volcanoes and tidal bores, make it difficult to explain, and without being thrown about by the limbs of any animate beings. It is often said that these objects behave in a way which exhibits signs of (usually mischievous) design.

I cannot see that the occurrence of such phenomena would strengthen (or weaken) any religious claims. The conceptual ideas suggested by the possibility of their being purposive, however, are interesting. For, if the phenomena are the product of some rudimentary mind, then control is exercised by this mind over inanimate objects without its first having to manipulate some object which is its body. If these objects are directed at any target with any accuracy, it must be able to detect the presence of this target without having receptor organs. This fact is worth drawing attention to because, if there is a God, he must exercise such a direct control over inanimate objects, and locate their whereabouts without eyes or other sense organs.

MATERIALISM

There are some reasons—which have, I think, been greatly exaggerated—for thinking that religious doctrines must be false if materialism is true. For example, if materialism is true, there cannot be a God, for in this case God's mind would be dependent upon or identical with his body; but God does not have a body. For the same reason, diembodied existence would be impossible.

I do not know that the occurrence of paranormal phenomena would constitute a knock-down proof that materialism was false. For example, the fact that an event in my mind is caused in a paranormal way by an event in yours does not prove that they are not physical events. The fact that I could sometimes successfully will a die to fall six-uppermost would not show that willing was not a physical event. One could, however, go on maintaining that these things were physical events only at the cost of allowing some very peculiar connections between physical events, which would make it less economical than has been supposed to maintain that all events are physical.

One of the most interesting features of trance-mediumship is that when, as occasionally appears to happen, the communicator speaks with the medium's lips, though he appears to take over her body, he is nevertheless not related to it as we are to our bodies. For our personality is supposed to be determined by our brain and endocrine balance. The communicator, however, retains his own personality, while operating with a body which has the medium's brain and endocrine balance. This would provide some evidence that epiphenomenalism is false.

FUNDAMENTAL DIFFICULTIES

I would like to end by drawing attention to some fundamental difficulties in the way of supposing that the study of paranormal psychology can have any bearing upon religion, or, at any rate, upon the existence of God. God is supposed to be a necessary being, and if this means or entails that he necessarily exists, the conclusion should be that no empirical contingent facts can follow from his existence, and so no empirical contingent facts can establish his existence. For a necessary proposition, which must be true, cannot entail any proposition which might be false, and all contingent empirical propostions might be false. Furthermore, a God who is postulated to explain certain empirical facts must be a God who is one item of furniture within the spatio-temporal order, much as the planet which was postulated (and subsequently discovered) to explain why the planets did not move as, according to Kepler's laws, they should have done. God, however, is not supposed to be an additional item on the list of things in the universe, but to transcend it. Postulating a God to explain the phenomena studied by paranormal psychologists would suffer from the disadvantages which Kant drew attention to in his criticisms of the argument from design—that the best it could show would be the existence of a very powerful journeyman, not that of an omnipotent, omniscient, transcendent creator. In any case, the facts, if we accept that there are any, are neither more nor less amenable to a teleological explanation than the normal facts; nor are they unequivocally indicative of a wholly wise and good creator, or unequivocally indicative of a wholly malevolent creator. If the existence of God is a hypothesis to explain, among other things, such phenomena, his existence can be confirmed by them, but so, too, can his existence be disconfirmed by them. Many philosophers of religion, therefore, wish to set the existence of God beyond the possibility of disconfirmation. The penalty for doing this is that you set his existence beyond the possibility of confirmation, in particular confirmation by the findings of psychical research, too. Faith in a God who was postulated partly to explain paranormal phenomena would also be difficult to explain. An empirical hypothesis ought to be accepted provisionally so long as the evidence is in its favour, and one should be prepared to reject it if the evidence, as it well might, tells against it. The idea that faith is a virtue in which one ought to persist in all circumstances accords ill with treating the existence of God as an empirical hypothesis, for there should be no reluctance to abandon these when facts are discovered which they do not explain. Indeed, the idea that postulating the existence of God might enable one to make detailed and checkable predictions about paranormal (or any other) phenomena is one so absurd that, so far as I know, no philosopher has ever taken it seriously. But if no such detailed predictions can be deduced from the existence of God, the scientific usefulness of such a hypothesis is difficult to make out.

If the alleged empirical facts *are* facts, what they point to more than anything else is a universe which contains more 'psychical activity' than occurs in the consciousness of normal minds; where the boundaries between one mind and another are sometimes indistinct; and where not all psychical activity is sufficiently organised, or part of a sufficiently well-developed whole, to enable one to insist that all psychical activity must be the activity of some one unitary mind. It points to a universe where some psychical activity becomes disconnected from any living organism, and where the one–one relation between organised systems of psychical activity (minds) and organised bodies does not in all circumstances hold. It points to a universe where man can to some extent transcend his senses, and also manipulate objects in a way not wholly limited by the capacity of his body; where man is not so much the plaything of his physiological make-up as study of the normal evidence would suggest.[3]

One moral of this should be not so much that there is in reality simply one mind, or more minds than there are bodies (though this may be true) as that the question, 'How many minds are there?' is not wholly clear. It is more like the question, 'How many waves are there in the sea?' than it is like the question, 'How many seats are there in Parliament?'. To say that what the evidence shows is that there is one underlying mind, let alone that this mind is omnipotent, omniscient and benevolent, is going far beyond any empirical evidence there is, even if we accept all the evidence there is at its face value. And, as I have already said, it may be that the question of the existence of God is one to which any amount of empirical evidence is irrelevant, one way or the other.[4]

NOTES

(1) See C. D. Broad, *Lectures on Psychical Research*, (Routledge & Keegan Paul, 1962).

(2) See H. H. Price, *Essays in the Philosophy of Religion* (Oxford University Press, 1972).

(3) See F. W. H. Myers, *Human Personality* (University Books Inc., 1961).

(4) For a fascinating account of the development of the study of paranormal phenomena, I recommend Alan Gauld, *The Founders of Psychical Research* (Routledge & Kegan Paul, 1968).

6

SOME ASPECTS OF THE
PROBLEM OF SURVIVAL

by

PAMELA M. HUBY

I shall be concerned here mainly with that aspect of the problem of survival which is connected with questions of personal identity, that is with whether, to what extent, and in what sense a post mortem entity could be said to be identical with a person who lived at an earlier time. I shall leave untouched the problem of disembodied existence, which has been treated at length by Penelhum[1] and touched on by Strawson,[2] contenting myself with saying that there seem to be impressive difficulties here if one thinks, for other reasons, that post mortem existence must be disembodied existence, but that they evaporate if one abandons this prejudice.[3]

The concept of personal identity has been discussed recently by a number of philosophers working on the 'Brownson problem' and its descendants deriving from Shoemaker's work.[4] This starts from a science fiction example: the brain of one man is transferred by surgeons to the body of another, and questions about the identity of the resulting 'person' are raised. With some elegance further possibilities have been explored, and the results have a clinical beauty which justifies the choice of method.

Similar problems can, however, equally well be raised from a consideration of certain cases from abnormal psychology and parapsychology, and I propose to start from these. Unlike the Brownson examples these cases are claimed to be genuine; it must be admitted that few are reported with the scientific care that such extraordinary tales require if they are to be generally believed, but if they are fictitious they are at least no worse off than the Brownson cases, and enable us to imagine a variety of possible situations. I shall give, with each case, a short account of its origins, and references to other similar cases. This is important, for I shall argue that the problem we are concerned with is at least partly an empirical one, to be settled by a consideration of the evidence. That evidence is often ignored, partly, I believe, because much of it is reported by people of little academic standing, and also because it is often grotesque, undignified, or comic. The latter in itself is not a good reason for ignoring it : much of real life is grotesque, undignified and comic. There may however be an underlying reason for caution with such evidence which is more important : if we think that what seems to us grotesque may appear in quite another light to the people who report these things, if they may regard them as satisfying or glorious, we may think that some kind of self-deception or wish-fulfilment colours their tales. But judgements of this kind can only be made on a full knowledge of the facts of what is reported and by whom.

Before we look at the evidence, however, something must be said about what the question at issue is. For many recent discussions of the problems of personal identity and survival start with an incoherent question : the writers seem to have in mind a model which does not fit the problem. Let us look at some of them.

(a) 'Could it not be imagined that the whole of one's existence was passed in a disembodied state? The objection . . . is that there would then be no means by which one could be identified.'[5]

But who is supposed to be doing the identifying? The 'one', or some other? And what is to be identified with what?

(b) 'If the having of E_2 and the having of this memory [of E_1] are *successive* experiences . . . the enterprise already collapses. If they are simultaneous, we face the distinct but equally obscure problem of what it is for two contemporary experiences to be experiences of the same person rather than of different persons. This seems to presuppose an understanding of what individuates one person from another, which is absent in the disembodied case. Many contemporaneous experiences occur in our world, and any two of them may belong to the same person and may not, and in the embodied world we usually have no problem in determining which way it is. But in speaking of bodiless persons, there seems as much problem in knowing what is to be understood by two experiences being experienced together by the same subject and not by two distinct subjects as there is in knowing what is to be understood by two experiences being experienced successively by the same subject rather than by two.'[6]

Here again we may ask, *who* is speaking of bodiless persons? *Who* is distinguishing between two experiences being experienced together by the same subject, and two experiences being experienced by two distinct subjects, and how does he have access to these experiences?

The problem can only be put clearly if it is seen as two related problems. One, put simply, is 'Shall I survive death?' The other is 'Have some people who once lived and are now dead survived death?'[7] These questions are obviously related, not just grammatically, as differing mainly in person and tense, but also inductively, in that an answer, or evidence bearing on one, is also evidence bearing on the other. But they are different questions even so, and the problems tend to get blurred if the matter is discussed either in terms of the first personal plural ('We') or the neutral third person singular ('One').

People who ask these questions may not be able to give a full analysis of their meaning, but they certainly mean something by them to the extent that certain conceivable situations would lead to the answer 'Yes', and certain others to the answer 'No', to one or both of them. There is room too for uncertainty, and that in two ways : some conceivable situations might lead some people to say 'Yes' and others to say 'No'; again, some situations (the same as, or different from, the first) might lead some or all to say 'The answer is uncertain.'

I propose to consider first 'Will I survive death?' To me, now, the evidence bearing on this must be inductive only : if others have survived, it is possible that I too will survive. But many writers have suggested that the whole concept of survival is incoherent, and that therefore it is impossible that anyone, including myself, should survive. I can try to meet at least this point in my present life.

Suppose it is possible (i.e. not logically impossible) that I should survive, it is possible that I should survive and not know that I was surviving. (This would perhaps be true of the dream-like state envisaged by Professor H. H. Price.[8]) It is also possible that I should survive and know that I was surviving. The latter is the more interesting possibility (and, unless in hell, the more desirable) and it is that that I want to discuss.

I start with an axiom : 'Anything that I experience, is my experience.' I call this an axiom, because I believe it to be true but unprovable. (At the same time, the history of science is littered with discarded axioms, so that I do not exclude the possibility that I might some day, through argument or experience, come to believe it false.)

From this it follows that any experience I may have after death will be my experience, and, if I am in a condition to think coherently, I will know (in a Cartesian sense) that I am having an experience, just as I know now that I am having an experience.

This point may be filled out by a reference to Wittgenstein : 'The world is *my* world . . . The world and life are one . . . I am my world (the microcosm) . . . The philosophical I is not the human being, not the human body, or the human soul, with which psychology deals, but rather the metaphysical subject, the limit of the world, not a part of it.'[9]

In these terms, survival for me is the survival of my world (the world of my experiences) with myself as its limit.[10] Wittgenstein here excludes both bodily identity and psychological continuity (in the sense both of memory and traits of character) from the metaphysical self. Modern discussions of personal identity frequently ignore the metaphysical self, but it is surely an essential element in what we are considering. As body and soul I am in my world, but so are many other things (all the things I am aware of); that world might continue to exist without my body—and, if out-of-the-body experiences are genuine, may certainly exist without its viewpoint being that of my body[11]—and might exist even without my soul (taking that, in Wittgenstein's sense, as that of which psychology treats), but it would still, in one sense, be me (I am my world), and in another sense have me, the metaphysical subject, as its limit.

Now it is conceivable that my world should shrink or become incoherent, as Price suggests it might, after the death of my body,[8] but it is equally conceivable that it should remain large, complex and fairly coherent, as it is now, or even better. This is surely a matter for empirical discovery. We do not know what the natural laws involved are, but that does not mean that there are no natural laws. If, according to natural laws, I survive death in the sense that my world continues to exist after my body has died, and that, while it no longer contains my body, the world contains enough of my soul for me to have memories of the past and the dispositional skills needed for thought, then there cannot be, for me, any doubt that I have survived.

When people speak of doubt in such a situation, surely the only thing they can mean is that I might doubt whether I was the same person as some previous person. I could not doubt my own existence at the time of doubting, but there are two possible ways in which doubts of a different kind might arise. Firstly, I might doubt whether the things I remembered had in fact been done at all, being then in the same position as a living person who doubts his own memories. In normal people such doubts concern only some memories and are caused by some difficulty about accepting them, such as that they conflict with other memories, or with what external evidence indicates was the case. A post-mortem survivor of the kind I have described would be in the habit of treating his memories in this way, and would be likely to doubt memories of his earlier existence only for positive reasons. What positive reasons there might be would depend on the kind of post mortem experience he had. It is idle to speculate about that at this point, but I do not see why methods of checking one's memories of various kinds should *in principle* be excluded.

Secondly I might accept my memories but still doubt whether the person who did what I remember was identical with myself. At this point I will say only that such a doubt might arise as a theoretical philosophical question, perhaps if I were, in life, convinced by philosophical arguments that post mortem survival was a logical impossibility. But such a question may be dismissed as parasitic. To ask, in this life, if I am the same person as the person who did the majority of the things which I remember doing, where there are no abnormal circumstances which might prompt a doubt, is to misapply the concept of personal identity. If it has application at all, it has it here. The only difference for a post mortem survivor would be if he were aware that he had died, and thought that this made a difference. If there were no other reason for doubt, doubt would appear to be unreasonable: if I now knew that I would survive death in the coherent form I am imagining, it would seem mere hair splitting to say that I might survive as a different person—or, perhaps, not as a person at all.

The argument so far has been that it is not nonsense to suppose that I might survive death, and that I might regard myself as the same person as the one I remember existing in life. Indeed, in certain circumstances I would be in no doubt about this. But the story is not complete without considering some matters which form a link between the first- and third-person aspects of the problem. I will therefore look at a number of examples from the literature of abnormal psychology and parapsychology, which taken together provide both some difficulties and some aids to the solving of our problems.

They fall into three classes: reincarnation, multiple personality and mediumistic communication. These phenomena illustrate different possible relationships between a present event or set of events and a past event or events. In cases of apparent reincarnation the question is whether there is identity between the 'occupant' of one body and the 'occupant' of a previous body; in cases of apparent mediumistic communication it is whether there is identity between a communicator, assumed to be only temporarily connected with the medium's body, and the 'occupant' of a previous body; in cases of multiple personality, by contrast, there is an apparent break of identity from one time to another, between the 'occupants' of one and the same body.[12]

Reincarnation
Fresh interest has been taken in reincarnation in the last few years because of the careful pioneering work of Dr Ian Stevenson.[13] By travelling the world with a tape recorder he has been able to produce a mass of material which suggests that reincarnation has

occurred in a limited number of cases. This fits in with some other cases reported over a century or more which follow the same pattern. Briefly, one person (A) dies young, either as baby, child or young adult, and shortly afterwards a baby (B) is born, sometimes into the same family but often outside it, which in early childhood reveals knowledge of A's life and claims to be A. In addition, B often has birthmarks corresponding to marks known to have been on A, particularly wounds inflicted at the time of death. In the best cases there is respectable evidence that B does have some knowledge of A's life and circumstances which could not have been acquired normally by B from relatives and neighbours.

Now B is undoubtedly a person, with a mind and body, and apparently remembers doing things as A. In some cases, particularly those where B is a brother or sister of the deceased A, who died in early life, no practical or emotional difficulties arise, and the identification can be accepted by all concerned. But in other cases circumstances may make it difficult for B to continue to regard himself as the same person as A, and then, as the child grows older, the memories of the past life seem to fade away.

A particularly striking case is that of Shanti Devi,[14] an Indian girl born in Old Delhi in 1926. At the age of three she spoke freely of her husband and children, and eventually said that she had been a woman named Lugdi, married to a man called Kedarnath, and living in Muttra, 100 miles away. Lugdi had had two sons, and had died the year before Shanti Devi was born, giving birth to a third child, which had survived her. After many inquiries, she was reunited with her previous family when she was eight, and behaved like a wife to the father and a mother to the sons who were in fact older than herself. But obviously this was an impossible situation, and, it is said, her 'husband' approached her with apprehension, not affection. As a result, she realised that she had to abandon her old life, rejected her love of her family in Muttra, and began to settle down as a normal young woman in Delhi, where she was still living in 1958.

Multiple Personality
In the early years of this century several well-known cases of multiple personality were studied, but for my present purpose the

most suitable is the 'Three Faces of Eve' case, which was made famous by book and film. As orginally presented, there were two alternating personalities, Eve White and Eve Black, later joined and finally replaced by a third, Jane, who seemed to her doctors much more mature and stable. But that was not the end, and later developments are told in another book, *Strangers in My Body*.[16] Jane was in fact still so inadequate that she tried to commit suicide, and this led to the emergence of yet another personality, Evelyn Lancaster, who not only had the body of Eve White, Eve Black, and Jane, but also memories of all their lives : 'Unlike Jane, who didn't obtain command of the memories of Eve White and Eve Black until after their deaths, I was born with an immediate full command of all my predecessors' memories.'[17] But, and this is the important point, she refuses to identify herself with any of them, regarding herself as having been born when Jane died. 'My memory of everything prior to the night before Thanksgiving 1954 is the memory of things Eve White, Eve Black and Jane did. Not I'.[17] 'The real story ends . . . when Jane vanished into the mysterious limbo where the shades of Eve White and Eve Black also dwell. For me, however, it was just the beginning, the start of a normal emotionally healthy, well-adjusted existence, the true beginning, in fact, of my life.'[18] These are Evelyn Lancaster's own words, and she maintains that her only emotional links with the earlier personalities are her love for the child that Eve White had had by a previous husband, and her happy relationship with the husband who had married Jane.

Let us compare the Shanti Devi and the Evelyn Lancaster cases. In both, there is a human being, in most ways quite normal. In both, there are memories of a past existence which, reluctantly by Shanti, but gladly by Evelyn, is repudiated. The difference is that while the personalities Evelyn repudiated were occupants of the same body as herself, the personality repudiated by Shanti had been the occupant of a different body. And for this reason there would presumably be different legal accounts of the situation. Evelyn Lancaster and her predecessors would be one person,[19] though perhaps a sick person not responsible for all 'she' had done; Shanti Devi on the other hand, would be a different person from Lugdi. But this account would not carry over to personal relationships : as far as we can tell, the decisions about themselves made by Evelyn and Shanti were accepted by, and acceptable to, their friends and relations.

These two cases, taken together, suggest that neither bodily continuity nor memory, separately or together, are sufficient to ensure personal identity. Other considerations may lead both the individual himself and other people to say that a new person is present, different from the old. This in its turn suggests that the problem of survival may not be simply the question of personal identity in a particular context. There was undoubtedly some connection between Evelyn Lancaster and her predecessors, and between Shanti Devi and Lugdi (if we accept their story): if it was not one of personal identity, it was still an interesting and important one, and one relevant to the problem of survival.

We have already seen that this problem involves matters of person and tense, and I wish to return to these here. Just as Bernard Williams asks questions about probable views of people about to undergo Brownson-type experiments,[20] so we may consider the probable views of the Eve personalities and Lugdi about what was going to happen to them. (This is not to cheat in quite the way I have discussed earlier. It is true that, on my present assumptions, neither could possibly have known what was going to happen. But if we accept my arguments about induction they, or anyone else, could be presented with various possibilities, and express preferences between them. With the growth of knowledge, it might even be possible to do something to achieve one kind of future existence rather than another.)

It is reasonable to suppose that Lugdi, who loved her husband and children, would view her future reincarnation as Shanti Devi with dismay. It is less clear about the Eve personalities: probably Eve Black would likewise have felt dismay about giving way to Evelyn Lancaster, but Eve White and Jane might have welcomed the prospect. But it seems likely that they would have had feelings one way or the other which would be different from those roused by being told, 'You will cease to exist. After that, somebody else will lead the following kind of life.' This suggests that one's interest in survival involves two separate aspects—whether one will exist at all, and whether, if one exists, one's experiences will be of a desirable kind. One may view with dismay both one's future extinction and one's future existence with undesirable experiences :

what one should welcome is the prospect of continuing existence with satisfactory experiences.

A complication arises at this point, however : it may be said that whatever Eve Black and Lugdi might be expected to have thought, in fact both Evelyn Lancaster and Shanti Devi were, in the end, contented with their lot. This is however a very general problem about the contemplation of the future. It is not even possible for a child to form a reliable judgement about the satisfaction he will obtain as an adult from a certain course of life; similarly, my judgement now about what I might enjoy in a post mortem existence may be very wide of the mark. We may put the matter at its sharpest by supposing that Eve Black and Lugdi would be aware not only of the kind of life that Evelyn Lancaster and Shanti Devi would lead, but also of the fact that they would be contented : what would they feel then? Perhaps the best answer one can give is that they would view the prospect with mixed feelings.

Similar things may be said of the third person approach to these questions. One may lose a friend in many ways, not only by death, but also by change of place, change of circumstances (such as great wealth) or change of personality. The extinction of a happy person whom one loves (except perhaps in old age) causes simple sadness. In the other cases sadness will be tempered with other feelings according to whether one believes one's friend will fare well or ill in the changed circumstances. And, as in the first-person situation, there may be other complications. The atheist may grieve both for his loss and for the facts when his daughter leaves him to become a nun, but he may also feel some comfort if he knows that she is happy. Similarly, those who contemplate the death and reincarnation of a loved one may experience a variety of different feelings. In the cases considered, there is the additional complication that they were regarded as peculiar. Even in India, reincarnation, it seems, is not taken for granted : crowds flocked to see Shanti Devi, and her former husband was flabbergasted by the situation; if it had been the kind of thing that happened normally, everyone might have felt differently about it.

Mediumistic Communication
So far we have been concerned with cases where, if we accept the

evidence, there is no doubt that the 'survivor', is a normal human being (Evelyn Lancaster and Shanti Devi), and it is from these that I have taken evidence about the 'first-person' problem. In mediumistic communications, on the other hand, there is considerable doubt about the status of the communicator, and so here we are concerned primarily with a 'third-person' problem, i.e. are these communicators, or at least some of them, identical with people who have died?

There is an enormous amount of published material containing mediumistic communication, and while much of it is of poor quality, both in actual content and in the way it has been written up, there remain a number of impressive cases in which there is strong *prima facie* evidence that the communicator is the person he claims to be. The mediums Mrs Piper, Mrs Leonard, and Miss Cummins all gave, over long periods, communications which were of high quality and were written up with care.

I take as an example the communications received by the Rev. C. Drayton Thomas through Mrs Leonard over a period of eleven years, ostensibly from his father and sister.[21] Drayton Thomas himself was convinced that he was in touch with the spirits of these people and that they were continuing their earthly lives, in the sense that they had the same personalities as on earth and adequate memories of their pasts, and he was able to converse with them as one might converse with relations and friends.

In this kind of situation, then, there is a human being, Mrs Leonard, who is supposed to be nothing but a vehicle for the communication of messages from other beings, which are not normally the 'occupants' of any living body—though in rare cases this may appear to happen when the 'spirit' takes control of the medium's body.[22] Further, these beings claim to have been in the past the 'occupants' of human bodies. We must now assess this claim.

I should first make it clear that a full assessment of this claim would involve a very long consideration of the empirical side of the matter. There are very good reasons for caution about accepting the claim of communicators at their face value, which cannot be gone into here. Fortunately, however, there are a number of excellent discussions of these matters, to which I refer anyone who is interested.[23] I shall here concentrate on the conceptual problem : supposing that we hold, even after examining the difficulties from the empirical angle, that there is still good *prima facie* evidence that Drayton Thomas was in touch with his father and sister, what more needs to be said?

Just as the 'first-person' problem of survival was connected with the problem of personal identity, so here there is a connection with another perennial philosophical problem, that of the existence of other minds. One might try to break down our problem into two parts: firstly, is there another mind here, and, secondly, if there is another mind, is it the same mind that was attached to the body of, say, Drayton Thomas's sister before she died?

The first question will be answered differently by different philosophers, according to how they view the problem of other minds itself. And I suspect that some of them, behaviourists, for instance, would have to come up with some surprising answers. But I must limit myself here to a discussion of the problem in the light of the analysis of the nature of personality which I have given earlier, in Wittgensteinian terms. The question then becomes: are we concerned here with two microcosms[24] (in the case of Mrs Leonard and Etta Drayton Thomas, the sister) or only one, Mrs Leonard's? (The further complication of the nature of Mrs Leonard's control, Feda, I ignore for the present.) On the dogmatic view that microcosms can exist only connected in the usual way with normal human bodies, there can be only Mrs Leonard's microcosm; Etta's microcosm must have ceased to exist when Etta died. If, on the other hand, we hold that evidence for the existence of an independent communicating system (something that can, for example, converse intelligently), with a certain degree of complexity and extending over a certain period of time (with or without gaps), is evidence for the existence of a microcosm, there is evidence for the existence here of a microcosm other than that of Mrs Leonard. It does not matter that appearances may sometimes be deceptive, as when there is a fraudulent medium consciously faking messages, or, possibly, a wicked spirit doing the same, because I am not claiming that we can in such cases, or *ever*, have conclusive evidence for the existence of an independent microcosm. It is enough that we can have something that counts as evidence.

On this view, then, there may be an independent microcosm here, claiming to be Etta Drayton Thomas. And the same may be said of the 'personalities' Eve Black, Eve White, and Jane. The attempt to dispose of mediumistic communicators and controls (like Feda) as 'just' secondary personalities of the medium does little to solve our problems. It is too easy an answer to distinguish between a 'person' and a 'personality' and say no more. For a behaviourist, indeed, there could only be a difference of degree between the two, but a nonbehaviourist needs to say what difference of kind he supposes to exist.

One possible answer would be that a person was conscious (a microcosm) and a personality was not, but this seems arbitrary, and in fact most psychologists, by the use of terms like 'coconsciousness' to describe a certain kind of relationship between personalities, seem to suppose that personalities can be conscious too. What reason, then, have we for calling the lively Eve Black, say, a mere personality rather than a person? There seem to be two : firstly, that she shared the same body with other personalities, and secondly that she was psychologically complementary to Eve White, so that the notion of a splitting of an original person into two personalities seems appropriate. If we accept this, we can regard the Eve Black microcosm as more limited than those of normal persons, but a microcosm for all that, and we may suppose that it came into existence at a certain date in 1931 or a little earlier, just as many microcosms come into existence, at least as far as most of us know, at some time round about the date of the birth of the bodies to which they are attached. What is more difficult is to give an account of what happened on 19 October 1953, when both Eve Black and Eve White 'died', leaving Jane in control, and again in 1954, when Jane 'died' and gave place to Evelyn Lancaster.

What continued to exist after 1954 were, it seems, Eve Black's body,[25] and Eve Black's memories, but not Eve Black. But even this may not be so. As we have seen, Evelyn Lancaster, with the body of all three of Eve White, Eve Black, and Jane, and memories of all three, yet decided that she was none of them, and gladly repudiated them all. But if we go back to Eve Black, and suppose she could have been given an intimation of what was going to happen, we might agree that she would be dismayed, but not be sure whether it was because she thought she was going to cease to exist, or because she disliked what was going to happen to her still existing self. We may argue that either answer is possible and conclude that we may say either that Eve Black's microcosm ceased to exist (at least as far as we know) or that it merged with others to form Evelyn Lancaster's microcosm.

The notion of merging of microcosms may seem obscure, but that is only if we fall into the trap of supposing that a microcosm is something like a physical body and obeys quasi-physical laws. That is not so. Physical bodies are public entities which can be placed side by side and traced continuously throughout a period of time. Microcosms clearly cannot be placed side by side (no one can 'view' more than one at a time) and in that sense are not public : it is also impossible to trace one through a period of time because, except to itself, it is not directly observable, and, equally, it is unable to 'step outside itself' and so observe itself independently over a period of time. So we cannot view the merging of two microcosms in the way we can view, either in thought or literally, the merging of, say, two drops of water. We may give sense to the merging of microcosms if we suppose that there may at one time be two (separate) microcosms, and at a later time be only one, with memories and characteristics of both the previous ones. It may then be a matter of choice whether to say that the microcosms have merged into one, or that two microcosms have ceased to exist but their memories have passed to a third, or that one has continued to exist and has acquired the memories of the other, which has ceased to exist. (And I return to the fact that 'what we would say' is an inappropriate way to talk. Identity questions are either for me about myself or for me and you about others.)

In passing we may look at the split-brain version of the Brownson problem,[26] in which it is supposed that a man's brain could be split, and each half implanted in a different body, taking with it the memories of the previous life. There would then, it is argued, be two individuals with identical memories but not the same as one another, and this disposes of the view that memory can be the sole criterion of personal identity. Transferring this to microcosm language, we may suppose that one microcosm (A) is succeeded by two (B and C), which both have the memories of the previous one. Now each of the later microcosms may believe himself, on the basis of his memories, to have been A. If B meets C, each may succeed in convincing the other that he has genuine memories of being A. It does not seem to follow, however, that both will have to withdraw the claim to have been A; nor that each, if he still claims to have been A, must deny that the other was also A; nor, on the other hand, need they be driven to the absurd conclusion that each is identical with the other. The fourth possibility remains, that they should accept it as natural law that this is the way microcosms behave, just as we accept that by vegetative reproduction we may get many 'identical' plants from one original plant.[27]

I have suggested that Eve Black, though in a psychological sense a mere secondary personality, could still be regarded as a microcosm. If so, then even if the communicator who purported to be Drayton Thomas's sister was likewise a secondary personality, she too could be regarded as a microcosm. If this microcosm had, as she seemed to have, memories of life as Etta Drayton Thomas, what good reasons are there, apart from the dogmatic one that this sort of thing does not happen, for denying that she was identical with the microcosm of the Etta who had once been alive?

Two *prima facie* difficulties might be put forward, both connected with the question of the uniqueness of a person. On the one hand, there might appear two or more communicators, through different mediums or even through the same one, who both claimed to be Etta and seemed to have memories of her life, but who seemed to be two different microcosms. (They might, for instance, both communicate at the same time, and say quite different things.) Alternatively, we might have reason to suppose that two communicators, Etta and John Drayton Thomas, say, were not independent, but aspects of one and the same microcosm. But even if we had evidence of this kind, all would not be lost. In the light of what I have said about splits and mergers there would be the possibility of, in the first case, accepting that there were now two distinct Ettas, or, in the second, that Etta and John had merged.

These fantasies aside, there may still seem to be something of the 'rabbit out of the hat' in my proposed solution, that if there is evidence for the existence of a microcosm, as good as the evidence we have in the case of living human beings (except that there is no body), and if there is evidence that this microcosm has memories of a past life, then it is identical with the microcosm of the person who had that life. But its strangeness could be reduced in two ways, by evidence and by argument. If very much more evidence of this kind were collected, and if people could freely go to mediums and talk when they chose to their dead friends and relations, views would change almost automatically; clearly we are a long way from that, but many people exaggerate the distance because they ignore the evidence that already exists. Alternatively, we may argue like this: the solution seems unsatisfactory because it is felt that some necessary element of the situation has been omitted. But what element is it? It seems we want something other than memory to guarantee the identity of the later microcosm with the earlier, but this is not, *ex hypothesi*, the body, what can it be? It seems like a hankering after a kind of persistent ego, other than either body or memory, but what kind of thing could this be, and what evidence about it could we ever have?

Perhaps, however, we should take a closer look at the notion of unconscious or subconscious mental activity. We do not need to be psychologists to know that even a normal person is not in complete control of the contents of *his world* (his microcosm). These contents are dependent not only on the behaviour of the external world of things and people, but also on an independent source of activity *in himself*. Both in dreams and in periods of absent-mindedness in waking life, something other than his waking consciousness takes over, and behaves at least moderately intelligently and intelligibly. Further, many psychologists have accepted the view that there exists a whole subconscious realm affecting each one of us, which is not to be regarded as being a microcosm or having a 'metaphysical I' at its limit, but which can in unusual cases produce a passable masquerade of an independent personality. On this view there would be only a difference of degree between the automatic responses we sometimes give in normal life and full-blown secondary personalities, including, perhaps, mediumistic communicators.

A mere theoretical difficulty about where to draw the line could be met in the familiar philosophical way, but a further difficulty is raised by some odd cases where mediums seem to have produced pseudo-communicators, in other words, communicators have identified themselves as being either people who never existed or as people who are still alive, and in normal health. The most impressive of these are the set of communicators studied by Dr Soal.[28] At some sittings with Mrs Blanche Cooper in 1921–2 he conversed not only with a character, John Ferguson, invented by himself between sittings, his thoughts being picked up telepathically by Mrs Cooper, but also with someone claiming to be the spirit of an old schoolfriend, Gordon Davis, whom Soal believed at the time to have been killed in World War I. Later it was discovered that Gordon Davis had at the time of the sitting been alive and actively engaged in dealing with clients. This case is particularly puzzling because a lot of evidential matter was packed into a short time (less than five printed pages contains the whole of the relevant conversations, including Soal's remarks and those of the control) and this included some things which Soal had never known, and, more puzzling still, a few items which were not true of Davis at the time but became true some time later.[29]

Now in the same series of sittings Soal appeared also to be in contact with his own dead brother Frank. But if the other communicators were not what they seemed to be, what of Frank? Could not he, like them, be the product of a dramatisation by the medium of material she obtained by telepathy? But the introduction of the term 'telepathy' to explain away mediumistic communication is not the end of the story. To begin with, in itself it at least half undermines the sceptics' position. Already they are admitting something difficult to accommodate in the traditional scientific and common sense scheme of things. But we may go further and ask what, on the hypothesis I am considering in this paper, is the relationship between telepathy and memory? From the third-person point of view, it is impossible to distinguish whether a living human being is using memory or telepathy (in cases where they seem to have accurate knowledge of the past) except by external means. And from the first-person point of view, a man himself may sometimes not know whether he has a dim memory or a telepathic hunch about something. This suggests that we may regard memory as but a species of telepathy—well-organised retrocognitive telepathy—so that the question can no longer be asked whether, when a communicator appears to have very full kowledge of the past life of the person he claims to be, he has that knowledge by memory or by telepathy. On this view,

Frank Soal remembered Frank's life, and he *was*, therefore, Frank. (To make the picture complete, evidence of Frank's personality as well as his memories would be required, but that too was present in some degree.) If this again seems a paradoxical claim, I would ask, as before, what more is required? Only more empirical evidence, not something quite different. What else could establish that in one case memory was present, in another only telepathy?

What perhaps is lacking so far is any account of the existence of microcosms in the intervals of our public time when they are not communicating with us through mediums. One stark possibility is that they do not exist at all. As we have seen, it is a mistake to treat a microcosm as a quasi-physical entity, which must exist continuously. Rather, just as my microcosm ceases to exist when I am in dreamless sleep, so the microcosms of communicators might exist only when communicating, or they might, perhaps, sometimes dream. Alternatively, they may exist in a 'full-blooded' way, as indeed many spirit-communicators claim to do. Evidence for such existence comes not only from the frequently disconcerting accounts of their present lives poured out through mediums,[30] but also from the 'cross-correspondences' which suggest that a group of members of the SPR were thinking actively and creatively and co-operating after their deaths.[31]

My conclusion is that the theoretical difficulties about survival are not insuperable. What is needed now is much more study of the facts.

REFERENCES AND NOTES

(1) *Survival and Disembodied Existence* (Routledge & Kegan Paul, 1970).
(2) *Individuals* (Methuen), 1959), pp. 115–6.
(3) Penelhum, op. cit. p. 104–5 speaks of the 'air of tasteless fantasy' that hangs over doctrines like that of the astral body, but adds later that 'reality may not conform to our theoretical or aesthetic tastes.'
(4) *Self-Knowledge and Self-Identiy* (Cornell, 1963), pp. 22–35. Another relevant discussion was inaugurated by John Hick in 'Theology and Verification', *Theology Today*, April 1960.
(5) A. J. Ayer, *The Concept of a Person* (Macmillan, 1963), p. 115
(6) Penelhum, op. cit, pp. 73–4.
(7) Some people also ask questions like: 'Has my pet dog Bonzo survived death?' I shall not discuss these here, but that does not mean that I think they are silly questions.

(8) 'Survival and the Idea of Another World', *Proc. Soc. Psych. Res.*, vol. 50 (1952), reprinted in J. R. Smythies (ed.), *Brain and Mind* (Routledge & Kegan Paul, 1965).

(9) *Tractatus Logico-Philosophicu*, parts of 5·62–5·641 in the translation of Pears and McGuiness (Routledge & Kegan Paul, 1961). I have substituted 'I' for 'self' in 5·641 to translate 'Ich'.

10 Similar points could be made in Kantian terminology, using the Transcendental Unity of Apperception and *the 'I think' that can accompany all my representations*.

(11) Of all paranormal phenomena, these seem to me the best supported by evidence. See C. Green, *Out of the Body Experiences* (Hamish Hamilton, 1968) and C. McCreery, *Psychical Phenomena and the Physical World* (Hamish Hamilton, 1973), Ch. IX.

(12) There is another ostensible type of paranormal phenomenon which involves an unusual relationship between present and past. This is exemplified by the well-known 'Versailles' and 'Dieppe Raid' cases, both of which have unfortunately come under severe criticism. Here the percipient, in 1951, say, experiences external events as they are supposed to have happened in, say, 1942. But his own part is merely that of an observer. He is not, in 1951, remembering *his own* experiences in 1942. This type of case is, therefore, outside our immediate sphere of interest.

(13) 'Twenty cases Suggestive of Reincarnation', *Proc. Amer. Soc. Psych. Res.*, XXVI (1966). A handy popular collection of cases is M. Ebon (ed.), *Reincarnation in the Twentieth Century* (New American Library Inc., 1970). See also C. J. Ducasse, *The belief in a Life after Death* (Charles C. Thomas, 1970), Part V. For a critical counterproposal see C. T. K. Chari, 'Paramnesia and Reincarnation', *Proc. Soc. Psych. Res.*, LIII, pp. 264–86. For *prima facie* evidence of reincarnation in an English context, see E. W. Ryall, *Second Time Around* (Neville Spearman, 1974).

(14) See Jane S. Singer 'The Return of a Woman who Died in Childbirth' in M. Ebon *Reincarnation* (see note 13) pp. 42–8. A complete documentation of the case is said to exist in Pondicherry. Much depends on its nature. A short account is also given by Ducasse, op. cit., pp. 245–8.

(15) Popular book by C. H. Thigpen and H. M. Cleckley, who also wrote the case up in the *Journal of Abnormal and Social Psychology,* vol. 49 (1954), pp. 135–51.

(16) By Evelyn Lancaster and James Poling (Secker & Warburg, 1958).

(17) *Strangers in my Body* p. 275. The style may owe something to James Poling.

(18) Ibid. p. 281. By contrast, the Real Miss Beauchamp spoke freely about herself as personality B I and as personality B IV. 'These different states seem to her very largely differences of moods. She regrets them, but does not attempt to excuse them, because, as she says, "After all, it is always myself".' Morton Prince, The Dissociation of a Personality (Longmans Green, 1905), p. 525. To illustrate the complexities with which we are

faced, and which cannot be explored in a paper of this length, I note that Walter Franklin Prince, the clergyman who studied the Doris Fischer case of multiple personality, and had spiritualist leanings, hints obscurely (*Proc. Soc. Psych. Res.*, vol. XXXIX(p. 281) that there were certain spiritualist features in the Beauchamp case which 'puzzled and nauseated' Morton Prince and were therefore omitted.

(19) It seems, however, that when a contract was drawn up for the sale of the joint life story to the *American Weekly Magazine,* it required the signature of all three personalities. (*Strangers in my Body*, p. 220.)

(20) 'The Self and the Future', reprinted in *Problems of the Self* (Cambridge University Press, 1973). There are other interesting papers in this volume.

(21) *Life Beyond Death with Evidence* (Collins, 1928.) A more recent case is in G. Cummins *Swan on a Black Sea* (ed. S. Toksvig), (London, Routledge and Kegan Paul, 1965).

(22) Mediumistic communications come in a variety of ways. Mrs Leonard was usually 'controlled' by a childish personality, Feda, who passed on messages from other entities. But other possibilities include periods in which the communicating spirit itself controls the medium's body, and 'direct voice' sessions in which the voice of the communicator is heard independently of the medium. For a lucid account of these and other relevant matters see C. D. Broad, *Lectures on Psychical Research* (Routledge & Kegan Paul, 1962), Section C.

(23) E.g. W. H. Salter, Zoar (Sidgwick & Jackson, 1961), Chs X and XI; Hornell Hart, *The Enigma of Survival* (Rider, 1959), Chs. 8 and 9.

(24) I shall from this point use Wittgenstein's 'microcosm', though 'self', 'consciousness', 'ego' are possible alternatives. Strictly, I should say, 'the microcosm with the metaphysical I as its limit', but as the two are interdependent this cumbersome expression is not used.

(25) It is noteworthy, however, that there were some minor but striking physiological differences between Eve Black and the other personalities. She, and she alone, got a rash from wearing nylon stockings.

(26) David Wiggins, *Identity and Spatio-Temporal Continuity* (Blackwell, 1967), pp. 52 ff.

(27) Wiggins, op. cit., discusses the possibility of there being a 'clone' of persons.

(28) *Proc. Soc. Psych, Res.,* vol. XXXV (1925), pp. 471–594.

(29) Another set of probable pseudo-communicators has been studied by Alan Gauld *Proc. Soc. Psych. Res.,* vol. LV (1966), 286–94.

(30) A well-known example is Oliver Lodge, *Raymond* (Methuen, 1916).

(31) W. H. Salter *Zoar* (see note 23) contains a useful account.

7

RELIGION AND THE
PARANORMAL

by

HYWEL D. LEWIS

There can be little doubt that, if some of the alleged findings of parapsychology could be established, they would have very great importance for religion. I hope to give some indication of this in due course. But first a word of warning. We must try to view these alleged discoveries in the proper perspective and avoid exaggeration and distortion. It has often happened that, when new discoveries are made, they are taken to provide a major clue to all remaining problems, the one key for which we have been waiting. A major fault of some philosophical systems, Hegelian idealism, for instance, or some features of linguistic analysis, has been to present themselves in this way. Process philosophy has lately been casting itself for the same role. In the late nineteenth century, evolution was supposed to be the open sesame, and we had 'evolutionary ethics', 'evolutionary social theory', and even 'evolutionary metaphysics'. Some turn to the teachings of Teilhard de Chardin in the same way. But it is extremely unlikely, in my opinion, that we shall find any marvellous once-for-all clue of this kind. Problems do ramify and they may be more inter-related than some have supposed, but they have also to be tackled on their merits. We must continue with 'the long and circuitous route' and resist the delusions of the short way.

One point at which this warning is very much needed, in respect to parapsychology, is where the findings of psychical research are invoked to counter materialistic theories or break down some other form of the alleged dependence of mind on body which rules out the possibility of some life after death. Many have rejoiced in the prospect of settling the issue of materialism and related doctrines once for all in this way. The day has dawned when we need not be troubled by these awkward doctrines any more—their spell is finally broken. But this is very false comfort. Materialism seems to me about as implausible a view as any we could adopt, and I marvel that ingenious thinkers still persist in it. I also believe that there are fatal objections to various forms of the 'identity thesis'. But this must be shown on its own account; if materialism is false, it must be shown to be so as a general account of behaviour and consciousness. If we fail to do this we cannot turn, as a last desperate resort, to psychical research. For, if a materialistic account of consciousness in general is plausible, it will not be very hard to extend this to the peculiar experiences and situations presented in psychical research. We must take the case for the nonmaterial character of consciousness on its merits; it must stand or fall quite irrespective of any particular finding of either recent psychology or physics. The appeal must be, for us as for men in times past, to what we find consciousness, in its varied forms, actually to be. We have no advantage here over Greek philosophers or any others. Experience itself must be shown not to be neutral here. If that will not do, nothing will. We must win the major battle and not allow our forces to be deployed wholly in a skirmish on the edges of the field and without proper support.

This being said, I must add, however, that those whose anxiety over corporealist views of personality stems mainly from the threat to expectations of afterlife, may well find considerable reasons for continuing to have those expectations in the findings of psychical research properly assessed. It will be unwise to proceed as if the issue rested solely on such evidence. If the corporealist views are sound, no amount of evidence will help. For, on that assumption, there could be nothing which could survive the dissolution of our corporeal existence. Some seek to retrieve the position here by extending their notion of our corporeal being, for example, to include an astral body. But, in addition to many other difficulties in this notion, there must surely be little point or comfort in the expectation that, when the body of which we are normally aware is reduced to ashes, an astral body, and that *alone*, will survive. Invoking the astral body will only help if it is allowed that a great deal more is involved. The idea of an astral body could indeed have significance if it were shown that strict continuity of our present material existence is essential for any thought of our continuity as personal beings. But it is also well to point out that the arguments for some kind of identity or other corporealist thesis rest on ways in which the body, as we normally apprehend it (affording a 'point of view' in perception etc. and causally affecting our mental processes) is vital, or thought to be vital, for an adequate understanding of persons and their experience. The astral body hardly comes into the picture here, and it is hard to see what function it could be thought to serve which could not be ensured equally well by some other body, an entirely new one which we might acquire or have conferred upon us. Indeed, much of the alleged evidence for the astral body could support equally well the idea of some different body or materialisation which comes about in special conditions. But even if there should be outright physical evidence for a properly physical astral body, or some like extension of our corporeal existence, this would seem to have little interest for us except as a means of sustaining more than an astral body in itself. To the extent that the astral body is a feature of our normal physical body or in some way continuous with it, the question must also be asked how plausible it is to suppose that the one can survive what seems to be such a total dissolution of the other. I will not pursue this further now, as I am convinced that those who entertain ideas of an astral body have not yet done their philosophical homework upon it. I return therefore to the main point that, with or without the idea of an astral body, such evidence as we invoke must relate explicitly to what we find ourselves, as experiencing beings, to be.

The substance of the evidence alleged to be relevant here, must consist largely, it seems to me, of ways we may be thought to acquire information which could not easily be explained except on the basis of its being communicated to us by persons who were once alive in this world but now dead. The form which this might take, and the stringency of the tests we should apply, have been considered in more detail by me in my book *The Self and Immortality*.[1] It is in terms of communications most plausibly attributed to 'departed' persons, rather than on eventualities of a more strictly or exclusively physical sort, that the most serious claims for psychical evidence for survival have usually been advanced. If some material component of me, and that alone, were shown to survive, it would not interest me more than some assurance that my bones were indestructible. To prove that conscious or intelligent creatures survive I need some evidence of their existence as conscious or intelligent creatures.

To examine the evidence we have in these ways for some kind of afterlife is too ambitious a task to be undertaken here, and it falls outside my scope. But it is not without significance that clear-sighted thinkers and investigators like H. H. Price have found the evidence in some cases sufficiently strong to warrant a firm indication of some kind of life after death. My own verdict, from a much more limited experience of the subject, would go the same way. If this is a reasonable view of the present state of these studies, then the implications of it are very great indeed.

Admittedly these findings of psychical research will not give the religious person all that he wants, or anything like it. The most that seems to be established is that some persons live on for some time after the destruction of the present body, though with a presumption, one might well suppose, that, after surviving so radical a change, the soul is not easily destroyed. Nothing is established about life eternal, and there is little indication of the quality of the 'life beyond'. Much that seems to 'come through', in mediumistic and other evidence, is remarkably trivial, although there is significant indication of a concern the dead continue to have for the living. But Professor Price has effectively pointed out that the appearance of nonsense or triviality in many of the supposed communications may be due mainly to complexities and imperfections in the mode of its transmission at present. It may not even be possible to convey to us, in the particular conditions of the present life, any distinctive richness of a radically different mode of being. But even if all this is granted, and if there proved to be nothing peculiarly exciting or inspiring in reports of a life beyond (and that is certainly too gloomy a view of the available evidence), the mere fact that there was distinct indication of there continuing to be life for us after we are dead—this would be quite momentous in itself.

K

That the evidence at present does not cause much of a stir is mainly due to the fact that, as in more popular accounts of hauntings and curious visitations, the reports are deemed to be too ambiguous and uncertain to be taken very seriously. They are thought to be stuff for the credulous and the uncritically pious. But if the evidence proved to be such that sensible people would have to accept it, or accept the substantial consensus of competent opinion, as we do in astronomy or medicine for example, then I find it hard to believe that this would not cause the greatest excitement, and indeed lead to radical changes of outlook.

This does not imply that the thought of a future existence is invariably agreeable. As many, including Broad and Price, have pointed out, it has its sombre and daunting side. Indeed, on some religious views, the fear of death is greatly inflamed by intimations of terrible punishments to be incurred when we come 'to face our Maker', unending torment as some Christians have thought in their curious commendation of the doctrine of a God of infinite love. Quite apart from aberrations of this kind, there are many ways in which the thought of another life, especially one whose quality will be much affected by what we have made of ourselves in this one, is daunting. Indeed any radical change makes us nervous and can be extremely disconcerting. The outright pessimism of C. D. Broad may be idiosyncratic, but he is not alone in hoping that we do not have to live beyond our present span. The prospect that opens before us can certainly be daunting. It has an unmistakably sombre side.

At the same time I am firmly convinced that the great majority of men would find unbelievable comfort in an assurance which they could firmly accept that their existence is not finally ended at death. The dauntingness of the change, and the strangeness of anticipations of life in some quite different mode, are not the root causes of the fear of death, but rather the thought of our total extinction. To pass out into the black night of total oblivion is a fate which is peculiarly dreaded, to the extent that the prospect makes a real impact, even with the further thought that we shall have no cognisance of it. The latter thought affords little mitigation of dread, and rightly so in my view. One's experience must be peculiarly jaded for us to take consolation in the thought that there is nothing beyond it. If, on the other hand, life has been found enjoyable and rewarding, if much has been achieved, the thought of further attainment and new experience and of fulfilment and enrichment not possible now, and of relief and compensation for many present ills, must surely be profoundly exciting and comforting. There should be nothing craven or cowardly in the thought of a life beyond.

I shall not pursue this further here. My view, for what it is worth, is that expectation of a future existence is a natural and proper one in itself and that the great majority would rejoice in any assurance of it. Indeed, if such assurance were unmistakable, that would not merely bring comfort to many, most of all at the death of their friends, but also open out new prospects and perspectives, sombre and exciting alike, that could radically alter our conspectus on a great many other matters and give us a more restrained and balanced view of our present fortunes. It would not give us all that various religions claim that we need, but it would give most of us a very new outlook and prospects which would substantially transform our attitudes and expectations from day to day. Life would not be the fleeting transitory thing which it seems to be for many. *Carpe diem* is not on any view a sound motto, and humanists know it well, they do not just eat and drink and be merry. But it does not follow that there may not be profound frustration for many at the limited and transitory character of present achievement.

The scriptures tell us of those who will not 'be persuaded though one rose from the dead'. This may be so as far as the profounder insights and transformations required by religion are concerned. But if anyone were unmistakably so to return, I can conceive of nothing that would hit the headlines more. And rightly. Far more would be involved than idle curiosity. The event might bring about a radical shift of interest, it would shake many to the foundations, and could perhaps work a major move forward in human affairs. Explorations of space might be nothing to it.

All power then to psychical research. It is not a panacea for all evils. Its potential is limited. But within its limits it could well have results, not merely of immense excitement in themselves, but far-reaching and profoundly beneficial for human society. Religious folk do ill therefore to look askance at, as very many do, or to fight shy of psychical research. They do well to insist that it is no substitute for religion, and that it does not come within its scope to meet the peculiar needs to which religion is addressed. It could well be that all, however fine and remarkable, could eventually defeat itself without religion. But there is no reason why psychical research should aspire to the place of religion, and it rarely seeks to do so. Religious people should not therefore look on parapsychology as a rival, or a dangerous pedlar of inadequate religious wares. They should view it, as many enlightened religious people do, as an ally capable of great achievements in a common cause and peculiarly helpful in a confused and sceptical age like our own. Indeed, nothing which markedly extends the range of human achievement and understanding is alien to religion.

As has been pointed out, however, the claims of religion itself are addressed to much deeper needs than those which can be met by psychical research, however novel and profound. The sort of phenomena of which we read in psychical research are those of clairvoyance, telekinesis, precognition, having dreams or apparitions which turn out to be of special significance, out-of-the-body experiences, etc. There is no inherent reason why any of these should not be understood in secular terms or admitted by a humanist. Even intimations of communications from the dead would not in themselves give assurance of more than an extraordinary extension of our own finite existence. This does not mean that we query the peculiarity of psychic phenomena as such or offer an account of them so attenuated that they are not paranormal at all. Nor does it seem plausible to me to account for paranormal phenomena exhaustively in terms of material conditions, as some would do. I believe such an explanation of any experience is in any case inadequate. All the same, we do not seem to have, in any of the alleged occurrences, more than remarkable extensions of the sort of powers we exercise normally.

Take causation at a distance. If I could lift the spoon at the far end of the table by just willing to do so, instead of walking round and picking it up in the usual way, this would be no more remarkable in the last resort than the control I normally exercise over my own body. It is just brute fact that I can change the state of my body in certain ways, and thereby bring about other changes. Explanation of how this happens is in terms of regularities in what we find in fact to be the case. If causal laws were different, or if we were endowed with different powers, these would be just further finite facts, and if they led out in some way to religion they would do so only in the same way in principle as any other fact of our experience. If we lived in a world of magic, as we might think of it now, there would be no more cause for wonder than there is already at the way we find things now.

The case is not substantially different, it seems to me, in respect to clairvoyance or precognition. If it is proved that some people do have such powers, this may seem very bewildering in relation to normal expectations, and it may baffle explanation. But this would be only in the sense that such powers do not fall within the course of what we normally anticipate. Would precognition be any more remarkable in the last resort than the fact that we normally see things when our eyes are open? We can explain the latter in terms of affectations of our eyes and in consequence our brains. But why should this extraordinary thing come about that we have this sort of experience when the brain is in a certain state? To this we can ultimately give no answer. If our powers were different, that might be very important in various ways, but they would still be exercises of finite powers.

In an earlier discussion of this subject, I drew a distinction between states which are paranormal in respect to causal antecedents or the way they come about, and those which are in themselves inherently different from what we experience in the normal course of things.[2] Lifting a spoon with a nod of my head would be very remarkable in the first way, in itself it would be the trivial thing it normally is. If I had considerable extension of such powers, this might have momentous consequences, but only by way of my being able to accomplish things I cannot undertake now, as someone who has learned to swim might rescue a person who would otherwise be left to drown. Acquiring a sixth sense would be a very different matter. I can form no idea what it would be like any more than someone totally blind from birth could have any proper idea of what colours are like. There may therefore be certain ecstatic experiences to which no proper analogy may be found in present experience, and of which no explicit account can be given to those who have not had such experience themselves. No one can deny that people do have such experiences, unless they claim that something inherently impossible happens, like seeing a square circle. There is no inherent reason why all experience should be the kind of thing we find it now, and if some people claim to have been lifted 'to the seventh heaven' or had some other experience of which they can give the rest of us no proper indication but only speak of it 'slant-wise', in terms of its conditions or accompaniments or in some very general terms from normal description ('wonderful', 'dazzling', 'horrible' etc.), then we certainly cannot rule this out in the sense of denying that they have had such an experience. They may have, but on the other hand we cannot accept this on their say-so. They may be lying, they may be deluded and not be having quite as odd an experience as seems to them. But the main point now is that, even if people do have experiences which are paranormal, in the present more intrinsic sense, this again does not in itself give us more than an extension of experiences which finite beings enjoy. We would have a parallel if most of us had been blind or deaf and some began to see and hear.

The mere fact of being paranormal does not, therefore, in either of the senses distinguished, provide anything of a properly religious significance. Everything will depend, as in normal experience, on the kind of paranormal experience it is. But this conclusion depends in turn, in some measure at least, on how the term 'religion' is understood. If everything which falls outside the normal course of our experience is thought to be religious, then paranormal experiences are obviously religious. In that case magic of any kind would be religious, and we might even find some persons apt to regard exceptional feats of science as religious—walking in space for example. There is no royal way of settling disputes about the meaning of a term like 'religion'. It is certainly used in a variety of ways and the list of possible definitions is a notoriously long one. But I should argue, however, as I have done at length in my book *Our Experience of God,* that the sustained and serious use of this term involves a reference to some ultimate existence in relation to which the fleeting and limited events of our finite experience find a more complete or abiding significance than they can ever have of themselves.

This may not require the sort of transcendent ultimate being, distinct from all other conditioned reality, which is prominent in most theistic religions. The case will be met, for some, in a monistic mysticism which accords a different role to seemingly finite things. But I should be prepared to argue that there must be a reference to some ultimate existence if the sort of aspirations we normally associate with religion are to be met. Postulation of another existence than the present one, or of the existence of beings vastly better endowed than we are and without our more obvious limitations, would not, I think, suffice, although some would find it odd to withhold the term 'religion' in such cases. My own view is that the aspirations men have in worship, prayer, meditation and all religious living direct us eventually to a transcendent being to which we stand in a special relation. What significance has the paranormal in that sort of context? It should be evident that, if the word 'religion' is understood along the lines indicated, then the paranormal has no explicit religious significance as such. It provides only further finite phenomena, and it is important that this should be stressed if the proper aims and conditions of a religious concern are not to be distorted, and energies directed misleadingly to wrong religious channels. At the same time, intimations of paranormal experience have had a prominent place in various forms of religion down the ages. This is due partly to peripheral affinities, and to false and superstitious beliefs and misunderstanding. But this is by no means entirely the case. We have to hold the importance of the paranormal in religion in the right perspective, but that is not to deny its substantial importance, in itself and historically.

Some of this may be discerned in the initial or basic insight by which we become aware of some supreme or ultimate reality on which all else finally depends. Such a transcendent reality is essentially mysterious and, in essentials, incomprehensible to us. We know only that it has to *be* as the ground of all limited and imperfect existence. But from the nature of the case the apprehension of such an ultimate unconditional being has no proper parallel in ordinary modes of reasoning or in other finite insights. It requires a very special insight which is itself evoked by enlivened apprehension of the essentially incomplete and conditioned character of everything else, including all that we encounter day by day. Such insight is aided and stimulated by those features of our experience which stir us out of the normal round and complacent acceptance of things as they are. Privations, untoward events, and disruptive experience, enrichment of experience beyond what we normally enjoy, these and like occurrences help to elicit the sense of a reality mysterious, not in the limited existence which baffles and amazes at the finite level but which is not inherently beyond comprehension, but in the sense of wholly imcomprehensible being; and among the evocative and disturbing modes of experience and occasions which have this character there must surely be accorded a high place to any paranormal experiences which can hardly fail to disturb the unquestioning acceptance of things as they are, and point to a reality which does not fit at any level into the categories of normal accountability. This must be a major reason for the prominence accorded to seemingly preternatural features of existence in traditional religion.

Religion rarely stays, however, at the level of an intuition or insight into the peculiar necessity of transcendent being. In oblique and mediated ways the 'beyond' which eludes our proper understanding in itself may be reflected in the limited world of our own experience in various ways which religious life and the study of religion disclose to us. Proper account of these intimations of God in present experience and history is a considerable topic in itself. But it should not be hard to see that considerable scope may be found for paranormal awareness to ally itself with these intimations and disclosures of God, and be brought into their service. It could well be, for example, that the glory of God is reflected in some distinctively enriching way in modes of existence and awareness surpassing those available to us now, but of which we may have occasional glimpses. As the expression of religious insights understandably takes markedly figurative forms, the peculiar mode of experience encountered in some paranormal states could provide new and stimulating symbolism for the enrichment and communication of religious discernment, and there seems little doubt that this is in fact extensively suggested in prophetic utterances and kindred expressions of religious awareness at diverse times and places. Affinities with art, both from the side of religion and the paranormal itself, will likewise be very extensive in this particular context.

A further feature of these phenomena which we need to heed very carefully is the possibility of distortion and perversion, and therefore the perversion of religion itself. We may allow the preternatural to impose itself unduly upon us and mar the balanced judgement of our present existence and its aims which we need to cultivate and maintain. Religion itself is peculiarly open to perversion, as the persistent warning against various forms of idolatry makes very plain. Religious practice has its dangers as well as its comfort and enhancement of being in particular, in becoming aware of the demanding, disturbing character of the impact of the transcendent upon us, we tend to evade it by diverting its rigour and splendour to related features of the media by which it is conveyed to us, thus, as I have put it elsewhere,[3] encapsulating the divine in the limited media, including our own religious roles and practices. Such perversion could in turn be aggravated and extended by its involvement in such preternatural factors as religion can most readily draw into its service, most of all if the latter are themselves abused or cultivated in ways at odds with the requirements of a rounded existence, whether in the furtherance of private aims or our commitment to one another.

At this point we have, therefore, a highly significant clue to much that is suspect in the history of seemingly paranormal powers and their association with religion. In unholy alliance, religion and the paranormal can be peculiarly and extensively harmful, and it is a gravely irresponsible matter to play with either. We may, or we may not, invoke actual evil agencies other than ourselves with which we may traffic or by which we may be influenced or corrupted, and there is certainly nothing inherently improbable in such possibility, but in one way or another, in overt demonology or less explicitly, we may find the preternatural in religion a source not of enhancement and illumination, but of peculiarly ugly and harmful perversion. *Tantum potuit religio sundere malorum.* Rarely is this more evident than in the present context. The remedy is not to forswear all concern with the preternatural but to achieve proper understanding of it and its place in a properly guided religious awareness. Though all our highest attainments admit of perversion, that is no reason for resisting them; we should merely exercise greater care in the direction of them to their proper courses.

A further topic to which these investigations relate is that of miracles. It is again notoriously difficult to indicate all that a miracle involves, but it is hard to use the term 'miracle' in a mean-

ingful way without presupposing some radical break in the course
of events as they happen in terms of the regularities we establish on
the basis of experience or observation. But such a break could
include much besides miracles—genuinely open choice, for example, and paranormal events. To constitute a miracle, there must be
not only the rupture in the normal causal sequence, but some
association of this with a supreme or transcendent reality on which
the finite order itself depends. How this is established is a further
issue in itself. But it follows, if my main submission is right, that
the paranormal as such is not expressly miraculous. On the other
hand, it would not be surprising if elevated and highly charged
religious states were to stimulate various paranormal powers which
might otherwise be dormant. In that case the study of miracles
and of paranormal powers might be found to throw much light
on one another.

Closely related to this are the problems of the peculiar claims
made by persons in various ecstatic states. These are also notoriously hard to assess, especially as the accounts that are offered
of them are in highly figurative language. Some claims, as in-
timated earlier, may be dismissed at once if taken at their face
value, for they seem to be inherently impossible. But the study of
other paranormal phenomena, including those which may be
deliberately induced by various physical stimulants or exercises,
could help us to understand better what in fact is being claimed in
ecstatic or visionary experiences. Study of the latter in turn could
help us in psychical research. The important point here, as in the
case we considered at more length at the start, namely evidence
for survival after death, is that the properly religious issue, however conceived, should not be straightway equated with that of
the preternatural as such. In practice the blend may be very close,
but that gives us all the more reason for heeding the appropriate
distinctions. Religion has to do, in most forms at least, with some
reality altogether beyond finite conditions, and the considerations
centrally relevant to it have little to do expressly with paranormal
phenomena. Religious life proceeds for many people without
thought of preternatural events, other than some relation mediated
in present experience with a transcendent reality, involving, for
most theistic religions at least, a continuation of our personal
existence. Evaluational considerations will have a central part in

this, and thoughts of preternatural events, including miracles if they happen, will be peripherial and subordinate to more distinctively religious concerns. At the same time, if these warnings are properly heeded, the religious person disregards the evidence for paranormal phenomena at his peril. He throws aside a peculiarly valuable aid in directing attention from the more mundane course of events, or the mundane view of them, to suggestive and stimulating aspects of experience which may be closely involved with properly religious insight, and may help to arouse and enrich it. Properly conducted, the study of alleged paranormal events could prove to be of inestimable value in the due appreciation of religious claims in a largely secular age. That could be exceptionally fruitful when religion is considered in close association with the study of art and literature. I would thus like to close my present discussion with a passage in which I summed up my own understanding of the subject in my fuller treatment of it elsewhere :

'The accounts we have of some supernormal occurences suggest very strikingly that they may have an exceptional suitability for the purpose of enlivening religious awareness and providing a focus for it. It appears from some reports of paranormal states artificially induced, and thus subject to more deliberate and designed inspection, that they involve a very sharp impact on the mind of real objects in one's vicinity or of hallucinatory ones. This has interesting affinities with art and religion and if these should be confirmed and seen to affect imaginative power in general, it would give us reason to expect exceptional states of consciousness to have a function, not unlike that of art and in combination with it, of focusing and sustaining and extending our religious life as a whole. But if this should be the case, we come back again to the integration of individual occurrences, however extraordinary, with our total religious impressions as they disclose to us the character of God and of His dealings with us which are much more vital for our relationship with God than any incidental feature of the setting in which they appear.'[4]

REFERENCES

(1) H. D. Lewis, *The Self and Immortality* (Macmillan, 1973).
(2) H. D. Lewis, *Our Experience of God* (George Allen & Unwin, 2nd impr., 1962), Chs XIV and XV.
(3) Ibid., Chs 3 and 4, especially p. 70.
(4) Ibid., p. 234.

8

ON THE 'PSYCHIC' POWERS
OF NONHUMAN ANIMALS

by

C. W. K. MUNDLE

I am going to discuss recent experimental work which seems to show that animals of various species can exercise so-called extra-sensory perception (ESP) and/or psychokinesis (PK). If this becomes well confirmed, it may alter the conception of the enquiry called 'psychical research' or 'parapsychology'. Richard Robinson once claimed that many psychical researchers would lose interest if they ceased to believe that the phenomena they investigate 'tend to prove the Platonic theory of the soul and man's survival of bodily death', and that 'at least some psychical research is . . . religion using science to try to prove its point'.[29] There is some justification for such comments, if we consider the declared purposes of the founders of the Society for Psychical Research. Referring to the formation of the Society, Henry Sidgwick said : 'We believe unreservedly in the methods of modern science . . . but we are not prepared to bow . . . to the mere prejudices of scientific men. And it appeared to us that there was an important body of evidence tending *prima facie* to establish the independence of soul or spirit which modern science has simply left on one side . . . evidence tending to throw light on the question of the action of mind either apart from the body or otherwise than through known bodily senses'.[38] He added later that 'there is not one of us who would not feel ten times more interest in proving the action of intelligences other than those of living men than in proving communication of human minds in an abnormal way'.[39] And the goal of psychical research for Frederic Myers is made plain in the title of his classic, *Human Personality and its Survival of Bodily Death* (1903), and in the Epilogue therein, where he writes of 'this great struggle from doubt into certainty—from the materialism and agnosticism which accompany the first advance of Science into the deeper scientific conviction that there is a deathless soul in man'.

The subject matter of psychical research ('paranormal' phenomena) is sometimes defined as phenomena which contravene established scientific laws. The Society's founders were not, however, concerned with all such phenomena. They selected for study such of them as seemed to provide evidence for psychophysical dualism, the thesis that the human psyche is an immaterial substance, not dependent for its existence upon the body. And not a few contemporary students of psychical research still hold that its main importance is that it provides grounds for rejecting Materialism. This view has been defended by John Beloff,[4] who wrote, in 1963 : 'there are, I believe, methods by which we can hope to isolate the psychic component of man, and it is just *this* that parapsychology, as an experimental science, is concerned to do' (p. 113). His argument for this conclusion is introduced by saying : 'there is one peculiarity of paranormal phenomena that tends, sometimes, to be overlooked : they almost invariably occur in connection with a human person. Now there is no *a priori* reason why this should be the case . . . But as it is, with the dubious exception of certain phenomena of the so-called poltergeist type and with perhaps the marginal exception of animal ESP, paranormal events are always bound up with people' (p. 111).

I am not sure what Beloff meant by describing 'animal ESP' as a 'marginal exception'. If he meant that there was (in 1963) no convincing evidence for it, I agree. Presumably he did not mean that animal ESP would be an unimportant exception to the generalisation that 'paranormal events are always bound up with people', since he interprets ESP as a manifestation of 'the psychic component in man'. In any case, evidence that rodents, birds and insects possess 'psychic' powers should embarrass those who have argued, like Myers, that men's exercise of such powers is evidence that 'there is a deathless soul in man', whose spiritual development will continue indefinitely. Would they draw the same conclusion about each rat, hen or cockroach?

I shall return to this question, but first I must indicate how I define and distinguish the powers in question. I define 'ESP' as 'acquiring information about, or responding appropriately to, people, things or events, without the mediation of any known kind of sense-perception'. Some have adopted over-ambitious definitions, which imply that ESP could never be conclusively verified. This was done in the *Journal of Parapsychology*, in September, 1957. Previously 'ESP' had there been defined, appropriately, as 'Response to an external event *not presented to any known sense*'. The revised definition replaced the phrase which I have italicised with 'not apprehended by sensory means'. This change seems to involve the error of assuming that 'known not to be so-and-so' follows from 'not known to be so-and-so'. I think that Tinbergen was not using 'ESP' inappropriately when, in 1965, he wrote: 'If one applies the term to perception by processes not yet known to us, then extrasensory perception among living creatures may well occur widely. In fact, the echo-location of bats . . . and the way electric fishes find their prey are all based on processes which we did not know about—and were thus extra-sensory in this sense—only twenty-five years ago.'[42]

Telepathy and clairvoyance are regarded as two distinct species of ESP. In the pre-experimental era, ESP was commonly classified as telepathic or clairvoyant according to the content of the information acquired thereby. The criterion now adopted is the presumed source of the information. The definitions currently given in the *Journal of Parapsychology* obscure the distinction between content and source. For example, 'telepathy' is defined as ESP 'of the mental state . . . of another person'. In practice, 'telepathy' is now normally used to designate ESP in which the information originates from (whether or not it is about) a mental state of another person; 'clairvoyance' to designate ESP where the information originates from (whether or not it is about) physical objects. (What is 'clairvoyantly perceived' might be overt behaviour or utterances which express a person's feelings or thoughts.) The above definitions of 'telepathy' and 'clairvoyance' are, I think, defective. The distinction is made to depend on whether the source of the information is mental or physical. But what right have we to assume that, where the information is about the unexpressed feelings or thoughts of another person, the 'agent', the source is not processes in the agent's brain? That all conscious experiences are accompanied and determined by brain-processes is a widely held hypothesis (or dogma). Only if physiologists could establish that certain conscious states are not correlated with any specific brain-processes, and we then found that the former can be ascertained by ESP, should we be able to verify the occurrence of telepathy as it is normally defined. If, meanwhile, telepathy is to be verifiable, it should, I think, be defined as ESP in which the information originates from the state of mind or the corresponding brain-processes of another organism. ('Organism', not 'person', to allow the possibility of telepathy involving nonhuman animals.) 'Clairvoyance' may then be defined as ESP in which the information originates from physical objects other than the brain of a living organism.

'Precognition', as it is used in psychical research, may be defined as ESP in which the information is about *and originates from* future events or states of affairs. The italicised words seem to make this definition incoherent, since it involves the notion of effects preceding their causes or of states of affairs which do not yet exist being objects of noninferential awareness. Note that the definitions of 'telepathy' and 'clairvoyance' imply that, in any instance, precognition would have to be telepathic or clairvoyant. The other 'psychic' power to be discussed is PK. This may be defined as influence exerted by the needs or wishes of an organism upon external physical processes, by means which are not understood.

I shall adopt the common use of 'psi-phenomena' as an umbrella term for ESP and/or PK. A question of some theoretical importance is whether it is possible for each of the species of psi-phenomena defined above to be experimentally isolated. In other words, is it possible to design experiments which could provide unambiguous evidence for each type of psi? By 'unambiguous' I do not mean 'conclusive'. Assessing the *strength* of the evidence for psi-phenomena is a task which I cannot undertake here. If we dismiss the possibility of precognition, on the ground that its implications are unintelligible (as I am inclined to do), unambiguous evidence for each of the other species of psi is obtainable with human subjects. An adequate test for clairvoyance is provided by J. B. Rhine's 'down through' method. (A pack of cards is mechanically shuffled and left face-down; the subject guesses the symbols from top to bottom, and nobody inspects the cards until the subject's guesses are completed.) And Rhine's 'pure telepathy' test is adequate. (No cards are used. At each trial, the subject guesses which symbol the agent is then thinking of. After the subject has recorded each guess, the agent records the symbol he had been thinking of.) If we allow the possibility of precognition, these tests are not unambiguous. In the would-be telepathy test, the subject might succeed by precognitive clairvoyance—of the signs which the agent writes down a few seconds later; in the would-be clairvoyance test, the subject might succeed by precognitive telepathy—of the thoughts of the experimenter when recording the card-order at the end of the run.

If machines can be trusted, it is easy to design a clairvoyance test which precludes precognitive telepathy. Let the subject's task be to guess the order of a series of numbers, randomly produced by a machine and recorded in a computer before the experiment starts. Let the correct guesses ('hits') be totalled by the computer, and disclosed after, say, each 100 trials, but without anyone ever being able to discover what number was the target at any particular trial. It is difficult to design an adequate test for telepathy which excludes precognitive clairvoyance. We may proceed thus. The order in which the agent thinks of the different symbols is determined by random numbers according to a code which the agent invents and never discloses; the agent alone checks the subject's guesses, and enters on each sheet only the total number of hits. This method is not proof against fraud and memory-mistakes but R. H. Thouless has suggested a way of reducing these risks.[41]

What about PK? In Rhine's early experiments, the subject willed dice to fall with a certain face up. But when the target to be willed was chosen by the subject (or an experimenter), the modest surplus of hits reported could be attributed to precognition. It is easy, however, to design a PK experiment which precludes precognition. Let the subject's task be to try to influence the output of an electronic random number generator (RNG), which number he tries to make it select being determined, just before each trial, by the output of another such RNG. If the RNGs regularly produced extra-chance matching, in, but only in, the presence of a person willing their correspondence, we should surely be obliged to ascribe this to PK. Now if we allow the possibility of nonprecognitive telepathy and clairvoyance, and of PK, it seems impossible to get unambiguous experimental evidence for precognition. It will always be possible to interpret the results of would-be precognition experiments *either* (i) by supposing that the subject's responses are due to unconscious inference from facts ascertained by nonprecognitive ESP, *or* (ii) by supposing that the events which fulfil the apparently precognitive responses are caused by the desires of the subject (or experimenter), by telepathic influence upon other people or by psychokinetic influence upon physical processes. It is normal practice in a precognition experiment to try to eliminate (i) by the following method. The subject records his guesses, e.g. of the future order of a certain pack of cards, and the targets are randomised, e.g. the cards shuffled, *after* the guesses have been recorded. But can we then eliminate (ii), i.e. the possibility of PK influence upon the randomising process, e.g. the machine, or the hands, which shuffle the cards? Apparently not, in view of experiments which I shall describe below.

In 1966, in a sceptical critique of psychical research,[11] C. E. M. Hansel wrote: 'An acceptable model for future research with which the argument (about whether ESP is genuine) could rapidly be settled ... has now been made available at the United States Air Force Research Laboratories' (p. 241). The feature of the USAF apparatus which led Hansel to say this was that the whole procedure was automated, that the apparatus 'automatically generated random numbers, registered the subjects' guesses, compared them with the targets and registered scores' (p. 170). The experiments with animals which I shall describe comply with Hansel's desiderata. Most of them have used a type of RNG designed by Helmudt Schmidt of the Institute of Parapsychology.[45] To explain how this functions, I shall describe the first experiment in which Schmidt used it.[30] This was designed as a test for precognition. The events which the subjects were asked to predict were each determined by a type of quantum process which physicists would regard as nature's most elementary source of randomness. From the subject's viewpoint, his task was simple. He sat before a display panel bearing four differently coloured lamps. His task was to press the button below the lamp which he guessed would light next. A fraction of a second after a button had been pressed, one of the lamps lit, which lamp lit being determined by the RNG which functioned as follows. A square-wave pulse-generator is continuously producing pulses at the rate of one million per second. Each successive pulse advances an electronic switch by one step, in the order 12341234 . . . When any one button is pressed, this brings into operation a delay-circuit which closes when the next electron is recorded by a Geiger counter. The electrons come from a strontium 90 source, whose radioactive decay involves emission of electrons at irregular inter-vals. The closing of the delay-circuit halts the electronic switch in one of its four positions and causes the corresponding lamp to light. On the average, electrons are emitted at the rate of ten per second, but the intervals between successive electrons are variable : it might be a millionth of a second (a 'microsecond') in one case and more than a second in another. This variability is the main source of the randomness of the output of the RNG, but not the only source—the Geiger counter fails to record about ten per cent of the electrons, and the frequency of the pulse-generator is subject to some chance fluctuations. So when the subject presses a button, it is not predictable in principle when the next electron will trigger the Geiger counter. Even if a subject knew the position of the electronic switch at each microsecond and could control the timing of his button-pressing to within a microsecond, he could not thereby control the RNG output, unless he knew to within a microsecond when the Geiger counter would next register an electron.

Schmidt's first experiment gave results which are statistically highly significant. The rate of scoring was only 26 to 28 per cent (for different subjects) against the chance expectation of 25 per cent. But in each of two series, involving many thousands of trials, the odds against the deviation being due to chance were about a billion to one. And in the second series, the subjects' task was to press a button below one of the three lamps which would *not* light. Subsequently Schmidt has done a variety of experiments with human subjects, with similar apparatus and similar scoring levels.[31-35] Two features of his first experiment should be noted :

(a) Although the subjects were asked to *guess* which lamp would light, one subject decided, in effect, to treat it as a test for PK. Instead of guessing, as he had done successfully in an exploratory experiment, he decided, in advance of the first main series, to press the button below the red lamp at each trial and keep willing it to light. He succeeded and his scoring level was somewhat higher than that of the other subjects. Clearly we have no right to assume that the success of the others was not also due to PK, despite the fact that their frame of mind was one of guessing. Presumably they wished their guesses to succeed.

(b) Schmidt recognised that it is essential to check the randomness of the RNG output, and he tested 5 million numbers so generated, most of them immediately after experimental sessions. In the many experiments subsequently done at the Institute with such RNGs, it has been standard procedure to test very thoroughly the randomness of their output, usually before and during, as well as after, the experiments. We are assured that such tests have always given the RNGs a clean bill of health.

Let us now turn to the work with animals. The term 'anpsi' is commonly used to cover both (i) the exercise of 'psychic' powers *by* animals, and (ii) the exercise of such powers by people *upon* animals. It is (i) with which I am here primarily concerned. Evidence for (ii) would not have embarrassed Myers—it would add to the repertoire of the human psyche. We must, however, note that there is some evidence for anpsi (ii), for we shall have to consider whether facts which seem to provide evidence for anpsi (i) can be ascribed to anpsi (ii). In the sequel I shall refer to anpsi (i) as 'Anpsi', and to anpsi (ii) as 'Manpsi'. The experimental evidence for Manpsi is not extensive, and none of it, I think, immune from methodological criticism. For example, Nigel Richmond has claimed to influence the movements of paramecia by willing;[28] W. Bechterev has claimed to get dogs to do what he wanted by 'direct mental influence';[3] Karlis Osis has reported some success in influencing the behaviour of cats placed in a two-choice situation.[23] Owners of dogs or cats would perhaps feel no qualms about supposing that the latter can tune in to their wishes by telepathy, but would anyone ascribe this power to single-cell organisms like paramecia? We can, however, attribute all such cases to PK by a human agent.

I shall now describe recent experiments designed to test for Anpsi. (Space does not permit discussion of nonexperimental evidence, e.g. what J. B. Rhine calls 'psi-trailing', i.e. cases where pets, usually cats or dogs, left behind after a removal, have found their way to the family's new home, after journeys, through unfamiliar country, of (in some cases) hundreds of miles).[27] I shall consider first what we may call the Schmidt method, since he introduced it.[36] He used a RNG of the design already described, except that the electronic switch was 2-way instead of 4-way. The output, a series of (let us call them) 1s and 0s controlled two 200 watt lamps. Each 1 switched lamp A on and lamp B off, each 0 switched B on and A off.[46] The RNG produced numbers at the rate of one per second. Lamp A was placed inside a shed; lamp B outside, performed no function. The air in the shed was at about freezing point. When a cat was put in the shed and lamp A was functioning the cat settled beside it, evidently enjoying its warmth. Schmidt's aim was to find if the cat's desire for warmth could so influence the RNG as to make lamp A switch on oftener than the expected 50 per cent of occasions. In 9,000 trials, lamp A was on 51·3 per cent of the time. The odds against this occurring by chance exceed 100 to 1. So Schmidt repeated this exploratory experiment. Not with the cat, which had acquired an aversion to the flashing lamp, but with cockroaches. These received an electric shock each time the RNG produced a 1. Schmidt's thought was that the cockroaches' displeasure might influence the RNG to reduce below 50 per cent the frequency of the shocks. To his surprise, in both an exploratory and a confirmatory series, the cockroaches received a significant surplus of shocks : 51·3 per cent in a total of 32,000 trials. Schmidt described this as 'psi-missing', by analogy with cases where human subjects trying (supposedly) to score high, get significantly low scores. But as Schmidt acknowledged by implication (p. 261), we need not suppose that the cockroaches were masochists! The results might be due to Manpsi, PK by the experimenter, and on the cat as well as the cockroaches. Schmidt did not divulge this, but probably, like most of us, he likes cats and dislikes cockroaches. The kind of 'experimenter effect' which is being suggested must apparently be taken seriously. There are grounds for thinking that an experimenter may influence his results paranormally (i.e. in ways which are not understood). For example, in an ESP experiment in which a group of subjects (humans) did their guessing in their homes, half of the sets of target cards were randomised by G. W. Fisk and half by D. J. West. The subjects communicated only with Fisk and knew nothing about West's limited role. But there were high scores on Fisk's targets and chance scores on West's.[44]

Successful use of Schmidt's method at the Institute has subsequently been reported with other species as subjects. None of this work has been published in detail, but I have seen reports which have been presented to the Parapsychological Association, and I shall summarise some of the results reported by W. J. Levy and others. The first step was to repeat Schmidt's experiment, using as subjects one- to two-week-old chickens, which need warmth. Lamp A was hung over the chickens, housed in a box with the air cool enough to discomfort them. This lamp was switched on by 1s and off by 0s from the RNG. Significant results in the predicted direction were reported.[13] The next step was to repeat this experiment using chicken embryos, eggs with a week left of their 21-day incubation period. The air around the eggs was kept at 96°F, the optimum for chickens being 99·6°. Four successive tests were successful, with an average rate of 52·4 per cent of lamp-on periods in 11,000 trials. When the air around the eggs was raised to 103°F, lamp A, as predicted, was on for significantly less than 50 per cent of the time.[14] The latest developments (unpublished) have used the same method to test individual eggs. Surprisingly consistent scoring patterns are reported : only about half of the eggs are 'highscorers', and when several high-scoring eggs 'co-operate' (are placed together below lamp A), the level of the scoring is raised; and when two high-scoring eggs 'compete' (one under lamp A and the other under lamp B), chance scores are obtained.[15] Lizards have also been used as subjects in an experiment of the Schmidt type. The overall results were at the chance level, but a significant difference was reported for different atmospheric conditions : when pressure and humidity were high, lamp A tended to stay off; and when they were low, to stay on.[43]

Let us now turn to what I shall call the Chauvin method of testing for Anpsi. This is unique in respect of the number of successful applications which have been reported. I am told that there have been twenty-three replications of Chauvin's pioneer experiment at the Institute of Parapsychology, only two of which have been unsuccessful. At the time of writing, nine of them have been reported in detail in the *Journal of Parapsychology*[16-22] and I have read three more reports which are awaiting publication. The animals used include mice, jirds, hamsters and gerbils. The American experimenters describe the results as precognition by the rodents, whose 'task' was to avoid electric shocks delivered to the floor of whichever half of the cage was selected by a RNG. The first such experiment was done in France by Rémy Chauvin, Professor of Animal Sociology at the Sorbonne. He published it under the nom de plume 'Duval'.[9] It was published in 1968 and was the first completely automated experiment with animals.

The experimental cage had a low central partition, over which a mouse could, and often did, jump. Each half of the floor was made of copper wire. The mouse's position at the beginning of each trial was recorded via a system of photoelectric cells and mirrors. At 60-second intervals, the RNG selected one side of the cage, and within 1/100th of a second an electric shock, which lasted for five seconds, was delivered to that side only, if and only if the mouse was there to receive it. Now in 1953 Osis had reported an experiment designed to test for ESP by cats, and had found extra-chance scoring only in trials where a cat avoided 'side-habit', i.e. its tendency to keep choosing the same side in a two-choice situation.[24] In the light of this, Chauvin reasoned that his mice were most liable to exercise ESP when they were displaying 'random behaviour'. He observed that, in most cases, a mouse remained on one side of the cage until it was shocked, then jumped to the other side, and stayed there until another shock made it jump again. This led him to eliminate, as 'non-random behaviour', two types of trial, i.e. changing sides after shock and staying put after avoiding a shock. However, he so defined 'random behaviour trial' (RBT) that it excluded also trials where the animal stays put after being shocked, due perhaps, he suggested, to fatigue. This left only trials where the animal had changed sides after a no-shock trial. In these trials there is no obvious explanation of the animal's behaviour, and Chauvin judged that they were most likely to involve ESP. The results conformed to this expectation. The overall scoring was at the chance level, but in the 612 RBTs (8 per cent of all trials), the average was over 53 per cent of 'hits', i.e. avoidance of shocks. Chauvin has successfully repeated this experiment.[10] While these experiments were in progress, the encaged mice were in a locked room and the experimenters in another room containing the RNG and recording apparatus. The construction of the RNG has not been reported, but the target series which it generated and was used in the experiments has been checked, and it passed the relevant tests for randomness. Chauvin ascribed his results to ESP and did not consider the possibility of PK influence upon the RNG. Does his design preclude Manpsi? It might be supposed that Chauvin clairvoyantly located the mouse by ESP and influenced the RNG by PK! This would be less plausible if Chauvin formed his conception of RBTs, and applied it, only *after* his first experiment was completed. Unfortunately the report does not make it clear whether or not this was so.

Of the twelve American replications of which I have read the full reports, only one seems to have been wholly unsuccessful. This was done by Schmidt, who used much stronger shocks than Chauvin, strong enough to make the animals hyperactive. In the work done by Levy with various coexperimenters, the electric current was minimal. It was adjusted for each animal to be only slightly aversive. In his first experiment, Levy improved Chauvin's apparatus. The latter had recorded the animal's position only at the beginning of each trial, so it failed to discriminate between cases where a mouse jumped (i) during the five-second shock, or (ii) during the fifty-five seconds following a shock. Levy's apparatus monitored the animal's position continuously. He claimed that this made it possible to identify many RBTs not identifiable by Chauvin's apparatus. He classified as an RBT any trial where the animal had jumped during the preceding fifty-five seconds.

In Levy's first experiment,[16] he used mice and jirds. Thirty-seven per cent of the trials were classified as RBTs, and of these 53 per cent were 'hits'. The next two experiments,[17] unlike the first, gave results which reached statistical significance, but the scoring level remained below 54 per cent. They led Levy, however, to discover a method of analysis which separated more effectively the successful trials.[18] Levy's reasoning was (a) that 'nervousness' as indicated by high frequency of jumping between trials is probably not conducive to exercising ESP, so he divided RBTs into 'high-jump' (three or more since the previous trial) and 'low-jump' (two or fewer); (b) that having just been shocked was probably not conducive to ESP, so he divided RBTs into 'after shock' and 'after no-shock' trials. Post mortem analysis showed that, in each of the first three experiments, the extra-chance scores were concentrated both in the low-jump and in the after no-shock RBTs. When these classes were combined, i.e. RBTs which are low-jump *and* after no-shock, the scoring level in each of the first three experiments was 56 to 57 per cent for such trials, and was clearly significant. And in the later American experiments of this type, this subclass of trials has consistently yielded the highest scoring level. Given that Levy's method of analysis was conceived after the completion of his first three experiments, its successful application to the latter suggests Anpsi rather than Manpsi. No one seems to have noticed, however, that Levy had changed Chauvin's use of 'RBT'. Chauvin's definition makes it self-contradictory to speak of 'after shock RBTs'. What Levy calls 'after no-shock RBTs' are what Chauvin calls 'RBTs'! Levy has, however, found that selection from RBTs (à la Chauvin) of those which involve only one jump between trials yields an appreciably better method of separating the high-scoring trials.

Consider four experiments published in 1973.[19, 20] These were computer-controlled. Handling of the animal subjects was thereby minimised—the inquisitive rodent entered the test-cage when the computer opened the door for it. The experiments ran unattended for several hours at a time. The results are shown in Table 8·1 overleaf.

In the experiments numbered (3) and (4) in this table, the experimenters sought an answer to the question whether the animals were 'getting their ESP information' from the electric current in the floor of the cage or from the RNG. For this purpose, they arranged for alternating runs employing two different conditions: (a) an electric current was delivered to the side selected by the

	Total Trials	RBTs à la Levy		RBTs à la Chauvin		RBTs à la Chauvin which are Low-Jump	
		No.	Scoring-Level	No.	Scoring-Level	No.	Scoring-Level
(1) Jirds	1972	613	58·2%	393	63·1%	324	63·9%
(2) Hamsters	1638	309	60·2%	196	61·2%	164	63·4%
(3) Hamsters	2287	522	57·3%	317	59·6%	236	62·3%
(4) Mice	1270	584	55·1%	389	57·3%	264	59·6%

TABLE 8.1

RNG, if and only if the animal was there to receive a shock, (b) a current was delivered to the side so selected, whether or not the animal was there to be shocked. These were labelled, respectively, 'the dependent' and 'the nondependent' conditions, because, in (a), the delivery of a current to the selected side is dependent on the animal's presence there. With both hamsters and mice there was high scoring—higher, but not significantly higher, in the dependent condition. The experimenters concluded that the animals can get information by ESP from the RNG.

If that is the conclusion to be drawn, this last experiment was superfluous, for all the previous applications of Chauvin's method used the dependent condition. The novelty of this last experiment was in trying the nondependent condition. Surely the conclusion to be drawn from it is this: *If* the results with the Chauvin method are due to precognition, a rodent *may* avoid being shocked by precognising an event of a kind perceptible by itself (electrification of the floor); may, but need not, for it may, in the nondependent condition, do what it must in the dependent condition, i.e. precognise physical events of kinds not perceptible by itself (or us), events like the emission of an electron or the resulting electrical changes in the RNG—the events which will determine that if the animal is on a certain side at the time, it will get a shock. If the animal's avoidance of shocks is guided by ESP, the latter must be precognitive. In the American experiments, less than 1/1000th of a second elapses between departure of an electron from the strontium 90 and a resulting electrification of the cage; so the animal has no time to respond to nonprecognitive

ESP concerning the randomising process. But does it make sense to attribute the rodent's behaviour to precognitive clairvoyance? This would imply that it can get information from the future states of the RNG, can 'process' the information and arrive, in effect, at the action-guiding proposition: 'If I stay on this side, I'll get a shock'! To make sense of the notion of precognition, we must, presumably, suppose that future states of affairs already exist, before they, or their effects, can affect our sense organs. Then, if precognition occurs, we (mice or men) cannot prevent events which have been, or can be, precognised. Then PK influence upon the output of RNGs must be ruled out as impossible. But the Schmidt method seems to have provided unambiguous evidence that animals can influence Schmidt RNGs. Surely we cannot have it both ways. If the output of such RNGs can be influenced by the needs of cats or chickens, we cannot also suppose that its future operations pre-exist to be precognised by rodents.

The possibility that the results with the Chauvin method are due to PK by rodents is discussed by J. S. Levin and J. W. Davis in a paper not yet published.[12] Hamsters were used in their pilot experiment, gerbils in the main experiment. In each series, there were alternating runs using two different conditions: (A) the animal's position in the cage was causally irrelevant—a shock was delivered to *both* sides of the cage whenever the RNG produced a 1; (B) this was the standard method, described above as the dependent condition. The authors describe condition (A), fairly, as a 'PK test', but describe condition (B), question-beggingly, as a 'precognition test'. They argue (*a*) that if an animal remains for long on the same side of the cage and thereby avoids shocks, this indicates PK. They assume (*b*) that if an animal avoids shocks in trials following jumping, this indicates precognition. But why assume (*b*)? A rational rodent which understood the set-up would not waste energy jumping in condition (A), it would just sit and *will*. But when the animals did their usual jumping, why should their desire to avoid shocks not have as much PK efficacy as when they are sedentary? The result of this experiment are presented as indicating that the animals succeeded in both PK and precognition. There is indeed a conspicuous difference in the results for the different conditions. In (A), the 'PK test', the gerbils' high scoring was found almost exclusively in trials preceded by no jumps, these, by definition, being nonRBTs, whereas, in (B), the 'precognition test', there were high scores only in the RBTs. I do not know how to explain this—unless as an 'experimenter effect'; it was what the experimenters were looking for.

I know of no attempts to repeat the Schmidt-type animal experiment except at the Institute of Parapsychology, but the Chauvin method has been tried elsewhere, with some success in two out of three experiments. Each of these used rewards ('positive reinforcement') instead of shocks. S. A. Schouten, a psychologist at the University of Utrecht, rewarded a thirsty mouse with a drop of water.[37] He argued that this should be less frustrating for the animal than frequent shocks, and hoped that evidence for ESP would be found in nonRBTs as well as RBTs. Contrary to his expectation, clearly significant scoring was found only in the RBTs, which gave a scoring level of 56·4 per cent, with odds against chance exceeding 200 to 1. What he classified as RBTs were trials where an animal changed sides, in a two-choice situation, after being rewarded at the previous trial. (It is not obvious that this behaviour should be equated with RBTs à la Chauvin, i.e. changing sides after receiving no stimulus). The fact that Schouten's results conformed with those of the other experimenters, and not with his own predictions, suggests Anpsi rather than Manpsi.

Two similar experiments have been done in the Psychology department at the University of Edinburgh.[25, 6] In the first, gerbils were rewarded with sunflower seeds. The scoring level for 421 RBTs (RBTs in Schouten's usage) was 55 per cent, and for 2102 nonRBTs was 52·1 per cent. Only when all trials were pooled was the deviation clearly significant (odds over 200 to 1). The other Edinburgh experiment gave chance results. These three experiments show that there are disadvantages in using positive reinforcement. The animals have to be trained to overcome their propensity to stay put after being rewarded, and the training was not very successful. A marked bias for a particular side was shown both by the Dutch mice (66 per cent) and the Scottish gerbils (71 per cent). In the Utrecht experiment there was apparently scope for PK influence on the randomiser which selected targets, but not in the Edinburgh experiments, in which the randomised target sequence was recorded on tape before the experiments.

What conclusions may be drawn from the dramatic development described above? Psychical researchers have not been accustomed to getting results as tidy and consistent as those reported in the animal work at the Institute. Have ninety years' efforts to pin down the elusive psi-phenomena at last hit upon readily repeatable methods of demonstrating them? Before this conclusion is embraced, the experiments in question need to be replicated, preferably by sceptics, in several more laboratories, with assurances from independent experts that the electronic devices are not responsible for the extra-chance scoring. But let us consider the reported results at their face value. I think that the Schmidt method provides unambiguous evidence for PK. In that case, success with the Chauvin method must surely be attributed to PK and not ESP; for here ESP would have to be precognitive clairvoyance, and the operations of a Schmidt RNG cannot be both precognisable and alterable by an animal's needs. And it is not only nonhuman animals which are reported to have influenced quantum processes. Schmidt and others have reported success in PK experiments in which the task of human subjects was to influence events determined by a Schmidt RNG.[1, 32-35] And, as I have just discovered, Chauvin published in 1965[7] an exploratory experiment, in which his subjects were challenged to influence, by willing, the number of electrons emitted by uranium as recorded by a Geiger counter. Each subject tried, for equal periods, first to decrease, and then to increase, the rate of emission. Five of his seven subjects produced chance results in both directions. Two, both 13-year-old boys, were conspicuously successful, in both directions. The results, for each of them, give odds against chance of about a million to one, according to the calculations of the physicist J. P. Genthon.

If we are obliged to accept PK as a *vera causa*, can other species of psi be 'reduced' to PK? Telepathy can be conceived as a form of PK in which the telepathic agent influences the brain-processes of the receiver. The standard precognition experiment can be interpreted as involving PK influence upon the randomising processes. (Admittedly this kind of interpretation is wildly implausible where the event ostensibly precognised is, for instance, the death of a friend, or an earthquake.) But we still cannot get a unified theory of psi, since clairvoyance is not reducible to PK. It is sometimes argued that PK implies clairvoyance. J. B. Rhine has argued[26] that success in influencing the fall of a die, by willing, implies that the PK must be guided by clairvoyant perception of the movements of the die. Rhine was conceiving PK on the model of perceptually guided actions, like threading a needle. This model is plausible when humans are trying to influence dice, for we know what *sort* of interference with a dice is required; but surely it has no plausibility at all when what has to be influenced is a Schmidt RNG, either by humans ignorant about how it works, or by cats, rats or chickens. Would anyone suppose that the latter could acquire, or interpret, the information needed to influence appropriately the RNG? We need not accept the view that PK must be guided by clairvoyance, but there is independent evidence for clairvoyance by humans. So far as I know, neither the Schmidt nor the Chauvin method has been adapted to test for clairvoyance by animals, but this can be done. Let the random sequence which is to be used for determining the target order be recorded before the experiment is done, and before the birth of the animal subjects if it is thought necessary to eliminate the possibility that they may succeed by exercising precognition.

If the facts force us to attribute PK to animals, is this intelligible? Not within the framework of physics. Still, at one level, it makes biological sense. The evidence indicates that the mysterious power is used to alter the organism's environment in ways which meet its needs, e.g. bringing the temperature nearer to the optimum. Such a power would have survival value. But if animals possess such a power, one would expect natural selection to have magnified it beyond the modest levels of efficiency indicated by the experiments. One might suppose that the physical force involved in PK is very weak, and that Schmidt's apparatus provides it with maximum scope. Presumably the force required to advance or retard by a microsecond the emission of an electron from radioactive matter is very small indeed. Such speculations cannot be pursued here. I must turn to the question whether Anpsi or Manpsi is the more plausible hypothesis for explaining the experimental data.

As the experimenters recognise, this question cannot be answered with any assurance, and it is hard to see how it could be decisively settled. If people have PK powers, one of the embarrassing implications is that when a scientist submits a favoured hypothesis to the test of experiment, his hopes would be liable to bias the results, whatever precautions he takes. Chauvin and Schmidt seem to have done their best to prevent 'experimenter effects'. In Schmidt's experiments with the cat and the cockroaches the trials went on through the night while the experimenters slept. But may we assume that people's wishes have PK efficacy only when they are awake? The Manpsi hypothesis looks plausible to the extent that would-be tests for Anpsi have given the kinds of results predicted or desired by the experimenter. But in some of the experiments—Schouten's, for example—the results have not conformed to their author's predictions. And in the Levin and Davis experiment, one eccentric mouse is reported as having remained on the same side of the cage almost continually and received no shocks at all; but it did so, disobligingly, not in a 'PK test', but in a 'precognition test'! Such cases suggest Anpsi rather than Manpsi. Schmidt's cockroach experiment also gave unexpected results, but Anpsi, implying masochism by the insects, seems less plausible than Manpsi. Perhaps the least weak point in favour of the Anpsi hypothesis is this. Experimenters who are in any degree consistent in getting significant results with human subjects are rare birds, and so are the successful subjects. More than a dozen experimenters have reported experiments designed to test for Anpsi, and only one pair have drawn a complete blank.[6] Assuming that there have not been many failures which have gone unreported, this supports the Anpsi hypothesis. If the experiments initiated by Chauvin and Schmidt do involve Anpsi, they *ought* to be readily repeatable. Chicken embryos are presumably less temperamental than 'psychic' humans; British cats and mice ought not to lack powers possessed by foreign specimens. So if nonhuman animals do possess 'psychic' powers, confirmation should not take another ninety years.

If confirmation comes, will this take the 'psyche' out of psychical research? I think most people would draw this conclusion. Other reactions are possible. No doubt Hans Driesch would have welcomed evidence for Anpsi as supporting his version of vitalism, according to which each living organism is controlled by a psyche, an 'entelechy', which is 'an agent *sui generis,* non-material and non-spatial . . . an agent, however, that belongs to nature . . .'[8]

But is vitalism a viable theory? If it were the only alternative to mechanism, and if mechanism had to be conceived in the manner implied by Descartes' philosophy, there would still be a case for vitalism. Acording to Descartes, all nonhuman organisms are simply machines whose behaviour is determined by their components according to the laws of motion; they are not even sentient, consciousness being an attribute peculiar to human souls (and God). Since Descartes' time, the arguments used to support vitalism have been arguments against Mechanism, designed to show that vital behaviour—growth, reproduction, etc.—cannot be explained in terms of the laws currently accepted as basic by physics. Most of these arguments have been undermined by progress in the sciences, and it would be rash to legislate about limits beyond which biophysics cannot develop.

Moreover, vitalism, as conceived by Driesch or Aristotle, is not the only alternative to mechanism. Another alternative is what I shall call the theory of emergence. This agrees with vitalism that organisms possess properties and powers not possessed by any inorganic bodies. It agrees with mechanism (i) that the ultimate constituents of organisms comprise only inorganic matter, and (ii) that the properties and powers peculiar to organisms are determined by the physical constituents and internal structure of organisms. It rejects the mechanists' thesis that the properties peculiar to organisms could, even in principle, be deduced from the laws to which inorganic matter conforms when it is not part of a living body. The emergence theory involves rejecting Descartes' conception of the unity of science—as a single deductive system in which the basic laws of physics function as the axioms. It permits evolution, in the inorganic as well as the organic realm, to be, in a sense, creative. For it implies that physical elements may, by chance, form compounds, which may in turn form more complex compounds, and so on, and that a new compound may have properties and powers which nothing in the universe previously possessed. It implies that some of the properties and powers of a type of compound substance, and the laws connecting these properties with those of its components, could not be discovered except by observing *this* type of substance. This theory permits the emergence, in creatures as complex as animals, of powers which are unintelligible within the framework of physics, e.g. powers to acquire and transmit complex patterns of 'instinctive' behaviour.

I am not recommending that scientists should abandon mechanism as a heuristic principle. To accept any property displayed by organisms as emergent implies that it is pointless to seek reductive physicalist explanations, but of course biophysicists must press on with their job. I agree, however, with C. D. Broad[5] that the emergence theory is certainly true for some properties, i.e. the so-called secondary qualities, colours, sound etc. When scientists have identified the physical processes in our brains which are the immediate causes of our experiencing each type of secondary quality, they can go no further. It will just have to be accepted as an inexplicable brute fact that, for instance, certain electrochemical changes in a certain part of his occipital lobe makes a man see a certain shade of green. That they make him see that colour, or any colour, could not be deduced from the physical properties of such cerebral processes. That is why a consistent materialist like J. J. C. Smart[40] wishes to omit secondary qualities from his ontology, and offers a behaviouristic account of what is meant by 'seeing colours', etc. Now if the emergence theory has to be accepted for properties with which all of us are acquainted, it may well be true for many properties of living creatures, including possession of 'psychic' powers.

I doubt if the philosophers and scientists who have defended vitalism would have done so if they had conceived of the emergence theory as an alternative to mechanism. I find it hard to understand the versions of vitalism with which I am acquainted. According to Aristotle, each plant has a 'vegetative soul', each animal has, in addition, a 'sensitive soul', and we humans have, in addition, a 'rational soul'. Sometimes Aristotle speaks of the rational soul as coming from outside, and as being immortal. But it turns out that he did not conceive of human souls as having *personal* identity after death. For he drew a distinction between active reason and passive reason, and held that memory and love belong to passive reason, which depends on the body, and that they perish at death.[2]

If anyone argues that Anpsi revitalises vitalism, he should not ignore the awkward questions which most vitalists have swept under the carpet. For example :

M

(a) Does he ascribe an immortal soul to every animal, or, if only to some species, on what grounds does he distinguish the haves from the have nots?

(b) If he holds that each individual soul originates in and perishes with a particular body and yet *controls* this body, how is this to be explained? Is God supposed to create and later annihilate each soul?

(c) Do his reasons for ascribing souls to animals not apply also to plants?

(d) Does consistency not require him to ascribe a soul to each spermatazoon, an organism which may live for several days?

Driesch dodged all these questions; unlike Aristotle, who held that a sperm ('the male element') has a soul which, if successful, moulds the raw material supplied by the mother. But, as W. D. Ross has remarked, Aristotle was silent on the question as to when reason enters a man's semen.

Reflection on the implications of vitalism will not, I think, encourage many to extend to the animal kingdom Myer's assumption that 'psychic' powers indicate possession of an immortal soul. Confirmation of Anpsi would seem more likely to alter radically the traditional conception of psychical research. The enquiry might be renamed 'parazoology'. If so, one would not, of course, wish parazoologists to study other species to the exclusion of *homo sapiens.* I rather hope that Anpsi will be confirmed, if only because it might do something to reduce human chauvinism and thereby curb our propensity to wipe out other species.

REFERENCES

N.B. '*JP*' stands for *Journal of Parapsychology.*
    'SPR' for Society for Psychical Research.
(1) André, E., Confirmation of PK Action on Electronic Equipment', *JP* (Dec. 1972).
(2) Aristotle, *De Anima,* 408 ᵇ24–30.
(3) Bechterev, W., ' "Direct Influence" of a Person upon the Behaviour of Animals', *JP* (Dec. 1952).
(4) Beloff, J., 'Explaining the Paranormal', *SPR Journal,* vol. 42 (Sept. 1963).
(5) Broad, C. D., *Mind and Its Place in Nature* (1925), Ch. II.

(6) Broughton, R. and Miller, B., 'An Attempted Confirmation of the Rodent ESP Findings with Positive Reinforcement', submitted to *JP*.

(7) Chauvin, R. and Genthon, J.-P., 'Eine Untersuchung über die Möglichkeit Psychokinetischer Experimente mit Uranium und Geigerzähler', *Zeitschrift für Parapsychologie*, Band VIII, No. 3 (1965).

(8) Driesch, H., *The History and Theory of Vitalism*, translated by C. K. Ogden (1914), p. 204.

(9) 'Duval (Rémy Chauvin) and Montredon', 'ESP Experiments with Mice', *JP*, (Sept. 1968).

(10) 'Duval and Montredon', 'Precognition in Mice: a Confirmation', *JP* (March 1969), pp. 71–2.

(11) Hansel, C. E. M., *ESP: A Scientific Evaluation* (1966).

(12) Levin, J. S. and Davis, J. W., 'A Comparison of PK and Precognition in Rodents', to be published in *JP*.

(13) Levy, W. J. and André, E., 'Possible PK by Young Chickens to Obtain Warmth', *JP* (Dec. 1970), p. 303.

(14) Levy, W. J., 'Possible PK by Chicken Embryos to Obtain Warmth', *JP* (Dec. 1971), pp. 321–2.

(15) Levy, W. J. and Davis, J., 'A Potential Animal Model for Parapsychological Interaction Between Organisms', unpublished paper.

(16) Levy, W. J., Mayo, L. A., André, E. and McRae, E., 'Repetition of the French Precognition Experiments with Mice', *JP* (March 1971).

(17) Levy, W. J. and McRae, A., 'Precognition in Mice and Birds', *JP* (June 1971).

(18) Levy, W. J., 'The Effect of the Test Situation on Precognition in Mice and Jirds', *JP* (March 1972).

(19) Levy, W. J., Davis, J. W. and Mayo, L. A., 'An Improved Method in a Precognition Test with Jirds', *JP* (June 1973).

(20) Levy, W. J., Terry, J. C. and Davis, J. W., 'A Precognition Test with Hamsters', *JP* (June 1973).

(21) Levy, W. J. and Davis, J. W., 'Introduction of an Activity-Wheel Testing Cage into Rodent Precognition Work', *JP* (Dec. 1973).

(22) Levy, W. J. and Terry, J. C., 'Further Study of the Wheel Testing Cage in the Rodent Precognition Work', *JP* (Dec. 1973).

(23) Osis, K., 'A Test of the Occurrence of a Psi Effect between Man and the Cat', *JP* (Dec. 1952).

(24) Osis, K. and Foster, E., 'A Test for ESP in Cats', *JP* (Sept. 1953).

(25) Petersen, S. and Parker, A., 'Precognition in Gerbils using Positive Reinforcement', to be published in *JP*.

(26) Rhine, J. B., *The Reach of the Mind* (1948), pp. 106–7.

(27) Rhine, J. B. and Feather, S. R., 'The Study of Cases of "Psi-Trailing" in Animals', *JP* (March 1962).

(28) Richmond, N., 'Two Series of PK Tests on Paramecia', *SPR Journal* (March-April 1952).

(29) Robinson, R., 'Is Psychical Research Relevant to Philosophy?', *Aristotelian Soc.*, Supp. vol. XXIV (1950), p. 196.

(30) Schmidt, H., 'Precognition of a Quantum Process', *JP* (June 1969).
(31) Schmidt, H., 'Clairvoyance Tests with a Machine', *JP* (Dec. 1969).
(32) Schmidt, H., 'A PK Test with Electronic Equipment', *JP* (Sept. 1970).
(33) Schmidt, H. and Pantas, L., 'Psi Tests with Internally Different Machines', *JP* (Sept. 1972).
(34) Schmidt, H., 'PK Tests with a High-Speed Random Number Generator', *JP* (June 1973).
(35) Schmidt, H., 'Comparison of PK Action on Two Different Random Number Generators', *JP* (March 1974).
(36) Schmidt, H., 'PK Experiments with Animals as Subjects', *JP* (Dec. (1970).
(37) Schouten, S. A., 'Psi in Mice: Positive Reinforcement', *JP* (Dec. 1972).
(38) Sidgwick, H., Presidential Address, *Proc. SPR*, vol. V (1888), pp. 272–3.
(39) Sidgwick, H., Presidential Address, *Proc. SPR*, vol. V (1889), p. 401.
(40) Smart, J. J. C., *Philosophy and Scientific Realism* (1963), Ch. IV.
(41) Thouless, R. H., 'Comments', *SPR Proc.*, vol. XLVIII (1946), pp. 16–17.
(42) Tinbergen, N., *Animal Behaviour* (1965), p. 44.
(43) Watkins, G., 'PK in the Lizard', *JP* (March 1971), p. 62.
(44) West, D. J. and Fisk, G. W., 'A Dual ESP Experiment with Clock Cards', *SPR Journal* (Nov.–Dec. 1953).

NOTES

(45) This laboratory was, until 1963, part of Duke University. It was founded in 1935 by William McDougall, and since then has been directed by J. B. Rhine.
(46) Here I have oversimplified. If lamp A were always switched on by the same signal, a '1', the results might be ascribed to bias in the RNG. Schmidt took the obvious precaution of having alternating periods when lamp A was switched on by 1s and by 0s.

9

EXPLANATIONS OF
THE SUPERNATURAL

by

MICHAEL SCRIVEN

It is now twenty-five years since I chose the above title for my doctoral dissertation at Oxford, which provides a conventional excuse for reconsidering the issue; but there are in fact some more serious reasons for looking at it. In particular, a good deal of further thought has gone into the theory of explanation since that time, considering only the philosophical perspective; a good deal has happened in parapsychology since that time, to mention the scientific perspective; and some very odd things have been happening in the physical sciences, which I believe establishes a quite useful comparative perspective.

I. THE LOGIC OF THE SUPERNATURAL

In one of its incarnations, Webster's Dictionary defines 'supernatural' as 'proceeding from an order of existence beyond nature'. Immediately, the difficulties are upon us. How are we to distinguish an order of existence beyond nature from an order of existence that is within nature, though perhaps very unlike many other things within nature? The lengthy efforts in other dictionaries take us little further. It seems that the only way one can make sense of the notion of the supernatural is in terms of a framework which distinguishes certain phenomena as supernatural because of their *exceptional* idiosyncrasy or *generic* differences from the other phenomena of nature. By far the most popular basis for doing this consists in identifying this class of phenomena as the actions (or the effects of the actions) of 'divine' beings. The distinction between ourselves and nature is ancient and easily understood and leads to the distinction between natural objects and artifacts, for example; and it can easily be extended so as to regard other beings with powers of control over this world as not being part of nature, either. Thus the universe is divided into the phenomena that proceed without the need for, or without being caused by, the intervention of agents—the natural order; phenomena that are due to our own interventions—the artifacts of science and civilisation; and phenomena caused by agents other than ourselves (putting aside for the moment the possibility that such agents were responsible for the whole universe), *some* of which we will identify as supernatural, namely those due to *divine* beings (as opposed to extra-terrestial ones). If this is a reasonable reconstruction of the historical development of the concept, and of part of its underlying grammar, then I think we must face the fact that to some extent the advances of parapsychology have created a kind of autonomous supernatural. For few parapsychologists today would regard telepathy or clairvoyance, for example, as manifestations of the activities of divine beings. We might say that there are two species of supernatural—the theological and the psychological. The theological supernatural is identified as the domain of miracles of various kinds; the psychological supernatural is the domain of phenomena so strange that they appear to deserve consideration as a second order of nature, but *not* one connected with the activities of divine agents.

But this is not quite satisfactory. It still appears to be necessary that some agency, human if not divine, be involved in the supernatural. For the behaviour and properties of the hundred particles of modern physics, with their qualities of 'strangeness' and 'charm', are at least as different from the properties of the observable world as telepathy is from perception. Yet we would not dream of referring to subatomic phenomena as supernatural. I suspect that the link with the realm of gods and demons has not entirely evaporated in our psychological uses of the term, as for example, when we talk about hauntings or poltergeists or psychic surgery as supernatural phenomena (possibly the term 'divining' is an indication of this bridge between the psychological and the theological supernatural).

The present issue does not simply affect the usage of the term 'supernatural', a term not much in vogue. Its significance is much greater—it concerns the whole 'ideology of parapsychology', the whole question of the proper scientific perspective on it. Over the last twenty years, there has been a powerful and popular line of argument amongst parapsychologists to the effect that psi phenomena are clear evidence of the falsity of materialism or physicalism. To a considerable extent, this argument reflects the same tensions that underlie our use of the term 'supernatural' today. On the one hand, it seems clear that parapsychological phenomena *are* extremely different from most of the reasonably well understood phenomena of conventional psychology; on the other hand, exactly the same thing was true of the properties of magnetism and electricity, relative to the physics of an earlier time, and is true of the properties of quarks and their cousins with respect to the physics of the 1900s. Hence, when we talk about telepathy as a counter-example to the doctrine of materialism, it is not clear how we can avoid being accused of a certain amount of parochialism; for materialism has managed to enlarge its content to absorb the novel phenomena of previous revolutions in physics, and it is not at all clear why it should be thought that this should not happen again, with respect to thoroughly substantiated parapsychological phenomena. In short, it seems hard to define materialism in any *logical* way, other than with respect to a particular historical epoch, so as to exclude a materialism which would fully countenance parapsychological phenomena. Putting it another way, it seems that the only materialism that can be really disproved by substantiation of parapsychologists' claims is *yesterday's* materialism, since the very act of substantiation demonstrates that the phenomena are indeed part of the material world, and hence that a current version of materialism must embrace them. Just the same kind of shift appears to occur with respect to the supernatural. As long as *strange* deities, bizarre and little-understood creatures (or personalities buried within ourselves) are involved, it seems to make sense to talk of the supernatural. But as we become more familiar with the split personality, with suggestibility phenomena, with hysterical afflictions, regressions, hypnosis, and psychedelic drugs and resultant experiences, then the very same phenomena seem to be classified as rare, aberrant, bizarre, abnormal, mysterious, or just interesting. Rhine and Pratt, who did not want to bring in exotic agents to explain psi phenomena, were *thereby* rendered almost powerless to show that psi refutes materialism, since *mere* strangeness (without nonhuman agency) characterises the particles of physics, which materialism embraces without difficulty—which indeed *define* materialism.

II   THE TYPES OF EXPLANATION

The location of the shifting sands of the supernatural is thus obviously affected by the power of our explanatory systems. And it is not just the possibility of explanation, but a question of what the explanation is in terms of, that determines the geography of the supernatural at a given point. For one might be able to identify certain phenomena as direct interventions by mysterious divine beings, beings who made the intervention out of—let us say—their love for mankind, though the exact nature and extent of that love is by no means clear, and almost nothing else about these beings is clear. In such a case, I think one would have to say that it is proper to call an account like this, which demonstrates that a certain puzzling event was in fact due to the deliberate intervention of a divine being with a certain motive, an explanation. Nevertheless, it would hardly show that the event was not a supernatural event—indeed, it would show that it was a paradigm example of the theological supernatural. So here we have at least one case where the existence of an explanation is not incompatible with the classification of a phenomenon as supernatural.

In the domain of the psychological supernatural, of the phenomena of parapsychology, the situation is by no means so clear. (Although I do not wish to argue that these two domains are mutually exclusive, the history of parapsychology has very largely been one in which investigations have been pursued independent of commitment to theology.) Now the nature of parapsychological experimental design—no more than the limiting case of ordinary experimental design—is such as to exclude 'natural' explan-

ations. That is, demonstrating that a parapsychological phenomenon has occurred at all requires showing that what occurred
was *not* explicable in terms of the entities in the pantheon of contemporary physics and psychology. If the phenomenon does not
succeed in clearing this first hurdle, then it is not regarded as a
parapsychological phenomenon at all, and what one says is that
one has 'explained *away*' an *apparent* case of communication
with the dead, etc. So it looks as if here—in the domain of
parapsychology—the existence of an explanation *is* incompatible
with the existence of a supernatural phenomenon.

However, there is no difference in principle between showing
that one has discovered a *new* natural phenomenon and showing
that one has discovered a *supernatural* phenomenon, as far as
the basic experimental design goes. The design is—can only be
—set up so as to exclude all *existing* natural explanations. It will
be clear from the preceding discussion that the only circumstances under which one might plausibly be said to have demonstrated the existence of a *super*natural phenomenon are those
in which one has met the criterion for showing that it is not a
natural phenomenon of the types so far understood, *and* also
shown that it is *so* 'different' from those so far understood that it
appears to be a case of 'another order of existence', *and* that it
involves some agent or personality. The problem that emerges in
fulfilling any such programme is that no differences in parapsychology appear greater than those in physics, and the mere
involvement of *human* personality hardly persuades us that we
should abandon materialism or naturalistic explanation.

Of course it is true that, even in the case where we give an
explanation that an event is due to divine intervention, our
paradigm case for the supernatural, there are a great many unanswered questions about, for example, the whole divine plan.
But this should not be taken to imply that one has not provided
a proper or complete explanation, for the situation here is no
different from the situation in the rest of science : explanations
only connect one level to another, they do not answer all questions about the level to which the connection has been made. In
fact, it seems to be an important part of the concept of the
explanation of the supernatural that there *should* be a great many
unanswered and very perplexing questions about the agent whose

action (or the effects of whose action) constitutes the supernatural event. It is for this reason that a merely human agent, no
matter how extraordinary his or her power may be, seems un-
persuasive as an example of the supernatural.

We seem to have identified fairly clearly two cases that are
connected with our topic; the case of explaining a supernatural
event as due to the intervention of a divine (though possibly
malevolent) being; and explaining *away* an allegedly supernatural event as being actually due to natural forces or factors.
The remaining case is the hardest one, and perhaps an entirely
ephemeral one. Can there really be any such thing as explaining
something like telepathy (or a particular telepathic feat), which
could still leave the phenomenon in the category of the supernatural? To put the matter bluntly, with respect to any other
cases besides the two already identified, is not 'explanation of the
supernatural' a contradiction in terms? If the explanation is in
terms of something well understood, then surely it would be odd
to describe the explained phenomenon as supernatural; if the
explanation is in terms of some entity that is not *at all* understood, then it seems to cast doubt on the legitimacy of calling it
an explanation. We might perhaps call it a partial explanation,
or an explanation of part of a phenomenon, but not a good
example of a scientific explanation. The one exception to this is
the case of an explanation in terms of divine being, and that is
not the kind of explanation now under consideration.

At this point, it may be helpful to look at some points from
the history of explanations in twentieth-century parapsychology
and physics, at least very briefly and superficially, in case they
provide some enlightenment for us on this issue.

III   THE LOGIC OF EXPLANATIONS
IN PARAPSYCHOLOGY AND PARTICLE PHYSICS

The development of science in the late nineteenth and early
twentieth century was by and large, but not exclusively, a
development of the range of implications of certain hypotheses
about the nature of matter that were steadily being revised but
which remained relatively few and relatively simply expressed.
It is true that in the history of the physical sciences we have had,

on various occasions, to add new forces to the basic set of axioms about matter, or had to modify previous hypotheses about the laws governing the existing forces. Each of these changes was to some extent a defeat for the cause, or at least the hopes, of scientific explanation. For the aim of explanation is to increase understanding, and understanding is typically increased by showing that the new or puzzling is really only a special case of the old and familiar, or of something very like the old and familiar which we can now see we have to accept as the basic reality. When a new force comes along, electromagnetic, gravitational, or the 'weak' forces of the nucleus, we make every effort to reduce it to the pre-existing ones; Einstein laboured mightily, and many followed in his footsteps, to try to develop a unified field theory that would subsume gravitation under an electromagnetic-gravitational system. Ingenious particle theories have been proposed that would yield gravitational influence as a special case. But the fact remains that all such attempts were unsuccessful, and contemporary physics is completely resigned to the idea that there are several, and not just one, basic forces. However, the number of these is not great; it appears to be either three or four. The situation with respect to entities, as opposed to their relationships, is far different. We now face a situation where the number of elementary particles is of the order of one hundred, and where the hopes of converting these into some modest subset of truly fundamental particles are rapidly receding. Is not the situation just like that which faced the chemists before the periodic table and molecular chemistry came to their rescue? Although that *might* turn out to be the case, an increasing number of contemporary physicists are inclined to think otherwise. The resistance to proliferation has gone down considerably, probably partly as a result of the failure of the defenders of determinism, and only partly as a result of the 'featureless' nature of many of the fundamental particles. The fight over determinism was a fight over explanation theory. Could one ever reconcile the contents of scientific physics with the acceptance of the inexplicability of certain clearly identifiable events in physics—for example the radioactive decay of an atom? Einstein and others argued that one could not; but physics has essentially united to reject that position. That is, physics has come to accept the existence of inexplicable events, without feeling in the least committed to the view that this is a deficiency in physics. On the contrary, it is held to be of the nature of the physical world that this should be the case. Nor is this just making a virtue of necessity : the von Neumann proof shows that an indeterministic quantum physics would have great difficulty in being a successful one. This blow to the conventional interpretation of physics as omniscient at least in principle has, I believe, been the principal cause of the relative complaisance of the physicist today. I do not mean to suggest for a moment that all attempts at successors to Gell-Mann's eightfold way have ceased to seem appropriate—on the contrary, substantial simplifications are properly and enthusiastically sought. But the sense that there must be a final reduction to, perhaps, the four quarks or to some other very small number of basically very simple entities certainly seems to have lost the kind of religious appeal that its predecessors had in the early decades of the century.

Now what has happened in parapsychology? Ingenious speculations of Mundle, Parsons, Thouless, Roll and many others constituted attempts to show that one needed only a single basic psi phenomenon, in terms of which one could explain the others by various ingenious reinterpretations. This was the kind of reductionist explanation that has traditionally been very successful throughout science. In these terms, the explanation of one supernatural event would be in terms of another supernatural phenomenon. But we have not achieved much success with the reductionist path : although possible in principle, independent confirmation has been lacking. I think the analogy with physics is exceedingly interesting. There is always a certain decision that has to be made as to the level of credibility of the evidence in various areas, but let us strike a moderately conservative balance and say that the evidence for psychokinesis is a little marginal, but still fairly impressive, that the evidence for the so-called mentalistic phenomenon of telepathy, clairvoyance, precognition and psychometry is good, too, and that there are another half dozen phenomena on the sidelines in almost as good condition, with perhaps a half dozen beyond that that may easily turn out to be as well off. While we could not be said to have 100 phenomena here, to correspond with the 100 elementary particles, this is partly a matter of how you define phenomena; and of course we can expect significant reductions in the particle field. Nevertheless, we must at least conceptually consider the possibility that in both fields we shall find ourselves with a very large number of basic phenomena that *cannot* be reduced to a small subset of 'absolutely' fundamental phenomena. What are the implications of this for science, and for parapsychology in particular?

IV   EXPLANATION AND DESCRIPTION

The only thing that one could say about physics in the light of the failure to achieve a massive reduction in the number of elementary particles would be that it was untidy. You cannot argue that it was unscientific, and—a more interesting point—you cannot argue that it is incomplete. It may or may not be the case that a reduction will later be achieved. This may in fact just be a world in which there *are* a great many fundamental particles.

In the same way, we may simply be inhabiting a world in which there are a large number of disparate psychological interactions. Of course, the scientific commitment involves the search for simplifying accounts of these, but it should not be thought that the reductionist programme has an indefinite claim on our time, any more than the deterministic programme has an indefinite claim on the time of the theoretical physicist. They have now essentially abandoned major efforts to salvage determinism, and it may well come to the point where they have to abandon major efforts to reduce the numbers of particles to less than—let us say—fifteen or twenty. Geography has not suffered as a result of its inability to reduce the number of continents, or to show that North America is really a disguised outpost of Patagonia! Reduction, in this sense, is not an essential part of science. Systematic objective description *is* such a part, and parapsychology may well turn out—like geography and perhaps particle physics—to be largely involved in that.

Interestingly enough, the two activities are not sharply distinguishable. There comes a point at which a sufficiently elaborate description, sufficiently documented and worked with for years, gives us the feeling that we have an understanding of the phenomenon thus described. We have not reduced it to another phenomenon, but that only offends our sense of aesthetics, and not our scientific sense. It is not even that there are legitimate questions to which we can give no answers. The question: 'What is the relationship of this phenomenon to certain specified other phenomena?' *can* be answered, but not as simply as if we could say that this is merely another manifestation of one or some of those other phenomena. There are many interesting relationships besides those of derivation; some of them are relations of analogy, some of them are relations of correlation, some of them are relations of coexistence; the study of the relations between gravitational phenomena and electromagnetic phenomena is quite illuminating on this point. To put the matter more precisely, it is a legitimate *aim* of science to reduce the number of fundamental entities (forces, etc.), but it is not a legitimate scientific *conclusion* to assert that there can only be a small number of these.

In abandoning determinism, physics did have to give up a certain self-concept. Prior to quantum theory, it seemed entirely proper to suppose that physics would one day be able to answer the question of why a particular physical phenomenon occurred when it did; and, relatedly, be able to predict if and when the phenomenon would occur. At least it was thought that this would be possible in principle. One may now, I believe, see that this was just another example of over-enthusiasm, analogous to that we have just discussed in connection with reductionism. That is, it is perfectly legitimate for science to *try* to predict everything, and to provide causal explanations for everything, but it was quite incorrect for anyone to have said that science, of its very nature, *must in principle* be able to perform these feats.

The properties of liquid helium are well known, and in the early days of cryogenics they were the source of much wonder. It is indeed amazing for us to see a liquid climbing up the wall of a beaker and filling it, to see it crawl up the inside of a fine tube with such enthusiasm as to produce a mountain at the top end, with no pressure differential to force it. What was this if not 'another order of existence'? The properties of plasma have proved so idiosyncratic that we now talk about a fourth state of matter, in addition to solid, liquid and gas. Is that 'another order of existence'? I submit that these are not regarded as alternative orders of existence, *even when* we have a real prospect of reducing them to laws and phenomena that we already understood. I submit finally that the only reason we have for regarding psi phenomena as disproving materialism or as the supernatural is the lingering aura (!) of exotic agencies. If we take psychology as being just as much a scientific enterprise as physics is, if we take the study of human behaviour, properties and capacities as just as legitimate a subject as the study of the behaviour of inanimate objects, then we will regard whatever humans do or can do as part of the natural order of existence, some of it more puzzling —and hence more threatening or more interesting, depending on one's insecurities and needs for security—than other parts of it, but all of it natural enough.

There remains the theological supernatural as the one *possible* domain for the subject, and here I would only say that the very attitude I have been supporting in the approach to parapsychological phenomena leads one inevitably to the conclusion that the status of the supernatural, which is here at least a conceptual possibility, is no more than that.

V   EPILOGUE

It may be thought that the position taken here is too strong to be sensible. Surely, it might be argued, there really is an *incompatibility* between the properties of psi phenomena and those of ordinary physical entities. Surely, it is this incompatibility that leads one to say that establishing the existence of psi phenomena demonstrates the falsity of materialism, i.e. of the doctrine that the world operates according to the properties of the more conventional material objects. This has been argued, e.g. by George Price (*Science*, 26 August 1965). It is, he pointed out, analogous to Hume's argument against miracles. But both those arguments are *themselves* far too strong. Both would show that no revolutionary theory in science could ever be accepted, since it involves overthrowing pre-existing and very well-supported theories. The weakness in these arguments is that they confuse 'evidence that supports a certain generalisation or theory' with 'evidence that refutes conclusions incompatible with the generalisation'. It is very plausible to identify these two, but the proper way to express the point is to say that evidence that supports a certain generalisation only counts against an incompatible generalisation or phenomenon to the extent that it *directly* supports the incompatible *part* of the first generalisation. To expand on this a little : it might well be argued that, at a certain point in the history of science, we have quite good evidence for the generalisation that the only forces operating on material objects were those of electromagnetics and gravitation. Then we discovered that other forces were necessary in order to explain the behaviour of nucleons; what happened? We do not say that there cannot be any nuclear forces, because of the previous generalisation. We immediately recognise that the previous generalisation reached out far beyond what was directly supported (and did so quite properly as long as there was no evidence to the contrary), but that its extrapolated version presented only a very weak *prima facie* case against the existence of other forces. *Direct* evidence of their existence simply overwhelms that weak extrapolation. The original 'evidence' for the generalisation that there were no other forces is easily handled by reformulating the generalisation more modestly as the claim that they are the *dominant* forces governing the behaviour of *macroscopic* objects. *That we really knew*; the rest we inferred—and when the evidence went against the inference, we withdrew our tentative and properly-drawn conclusions. The same applies to miracles, the supernatural, and the death of materialism. If miracles are shown to occur, then our extrapolations about the laws of nature are shown to be false, that is, our claims that these are all there are; but not a more circumspect formulation of those laws. Hence, we cannot argue from the strength of the evidence that *strongly* supports the *circumspect* formulation to the falsity of the evidence for miracles. And precisely the same argument, which is in this application enlisted in support of the reality of the psi phenomenon, applies to the attempts by parapsychologists to refute the doctrine of materialism. A modest reformulation of that doctrine is immune to the critique. When one gets down to saying exactly what the incompatibilities between 'science' and ESP *are*, as C. D. Broad and Price tried to do, it becomes very clear that the only clash is between very loose and far-reaching *extrapolations* from the well-established scientific laws, and ESP. (See Meehl and Scriven, 'Compatibility of

Science and ESP', *Science*, *132*, 1956, p. 14.) In short, the evidence that so well supports scientific laws cannot be appealed to in order to refute ESP. All it does is to establish a weak *prima facie* case against it—which amounts to saying 'Do not believe in ESP *unless* you have some direct evidence for it.' And, of course, we *do* have direct evidence for it.

Finally, let us briefly consider another of the puzzles about explanation and ESP. Richard Robinson once complained that parapsychologists thought they were explaining something by labelling it 'telepathy', whereas, he said, labelling something 'telepathy' is simply to say that it cannot be explained. Here's another example of an attempt to dispose of the supernatural or the parapsychological by a piece of logical legerdemain. Again, it will illustrate the extent to which a better understanding of the theory of explanation can enable one to cope with apparent conceptual difficulties in this area. Contrary to Robinson's view, it is—in certain contexts—perfectly appropriate for somebody to offer as an explanation of a puzzling phenomenon the hypothesis that it is due to telepathy; by this he or she means to convey the fact that transfer of information is occurring other than by the typical means, and the existence of this information in the mind of some individual associated with the experimenter is a necessary condition for success. There is plenty of meat in this hypothesis—meat that can be tested. For example, it denies that ordinary sensory transfer is occurring, and it denies that clairvoyance would be an adequate explanation of the events. On the other hand, of course, it does not provide a theory of telepathy itself. To explain a remarkable performance by a stage mentalist, by saying that he memorises a list of key words, may be perfectly legitimate, even though one cannot give an explanation of the phenomenon of memory. Explanations all come to an end; explanations all leave other things unexplained. Explanations of telepathy are perfectly legitimate, even though telepathy is not explained.

What I have been arguing for recurrently in this paper involves two theses. The first might be called the thesis of the slipperiness of the supernatural. If one looks at the history of the concept of 'action at a distance' in physics, one discovers that it begins by being abjured, that it was then established as existing in just

N

the sense in which it had been denied that it could exist (by demonstrating magnetic action across a vacuum), and that the concept was subsequently redefined so that it was *still* abjured, but the 'it' had changed (it was redefined as *instantaneous* action at a distance). In this way, one manages to retain a sense of indignation about something, even though the original justification for the indignation has turned out to be nonexistent. The same applies to the supernatural and materialism. One has to be fairly quick on one's feet in order to avoid simply making points against cast-off versions of a doctrine. The survival of the same verbal form should not mislead us into supposing that there has been no substantial shift in the underlying commitment. Countries may call themselves democracies or republics when almost nothing is left of the social system of the paradigm case of these forms of government. Similarly, as parapsychology—or quantum physics, or hypnosis—enlarges our perspective on the universe, a real change is occurring, even if we still continue to utter the same old formulas with confidence; 'physics does not believe in action at a distance', or 'rational people do not believe in the supernatural', or 'enlightened students of parapsychology realise that it refutes materialism' may continue to be supported as slogans—but their real significance has greatly changed, so much so that just as good a case can be made for rejecting them. In such a situation, it is better to bypass the squabbles over the slogans and investigate more specific issues.

The second thesis might be called the doctrine of explanation by assimilation. The proper first move in the scientific explanation of a novel phenomenon is reduction of it to pre-existing and well-understood ones. But of course this does not always work—it can never *always* work since there has to be at least one basic phenomenon for which it will not work. We are facing a situation in physics and parapsychology where it may fail on an unprecedented scale. But that is no limitation of science, only of simplicity. What is irreducible is not thereby inexplicable. This situation may require us to turn from 'vertical explanation' (derivation) to 'horizontal explanation' (analogy, correlation, etc.); but we may finally and correctly come to understand the new phenomena, the old supernatural, just as well as any other fundamental phenomenon.

IO

TELEPATHY, EVOLUTION
AND DUALISM

by

SHIVESH C. THAKUR

I

Constructive philosophical 'theorising' is nowhere more difficult or hazardous than in the field of ESP phenomena, for here one is never quite sure what the facts or preliminary data are. In saying this I am not simply referring to the denial by sceptics that there are any such phenomena. Even those who are generally sympathetic to the claims of psychical research may, with good reason, wonder which one—telepathy, clairvoyance, psychokinesis or precognition—is the irreducible primary principle (process?) of which the others are secondary manifestations. Until Rhine performed his DT (down through) experiments with cards, clairvoyance was often regarded as telepathy where the subject acquired information about a physical object or event by 'culling' it from the agent's mind, which itself happened to have got it through normal sensori-motor means. With the success of experiments purporting to establish psychokinesis, it is being suggested that so-called telepathy is really only psychokinesis where the subject does not 'read' certain thoughts of the agent but 'causes' him to have these thoughts. But, once again, it is in principle possible to interpret all evidence for psychokinesis as really being evidence for precognition. Perhaps the present state of parapsychology is not too unlike that of the philosophy of perception a decade ago, of which Gilbert Ryle is said to have remarked, 'it isn't only in the melting-pot—it's in it upside down'.[1]

But until suggestions to the contrary have been firmly established as facts, it is fairly safe to regard telepathy as an irreducible datum requiring philosophical–theoretical explanation. It is possible to take the view that telepathy is simply a statistical phenomenon,[2] that is, the scores achieved by successful subjects in, say, the Soal–Goldney or Rhine–Pratt card-guessing experiments are not so much 'evidence for' a form of communication known as telepathy, but that so-called telepathy is no more than the 'factor' that causes these interesting and puzzling scores. Telepathy is not 'communication' in any recognised sense of the term, since the subject is not aware of being in communication with the agent whose thoughts he is trying to guess; he simply ticks certain numbers on a piece of paper which turn out (by a margin of a certain percentage point over mean chance expectation) to be the numbers symbolically representing certain pictures that the agent was supposedly concentrating on at a specified time. This coincidence, it might be argued, is what we call telepathy.

Such a view is utterly noncommittal in respect of questions about the origin and mechanics of telepathy and, consequently, is neutral on the issue whether materialism or immaterialism, mechanism, 'emergentism' or vitalism provide the most satisfactory philosophical framework for the explanation of telepathy. Whatever the methodological advantages of such a view, however, it has to be said that it ignores the fact that the experiments in question were designed to test a given hypothesis explicitly stated in the definition of telepathy widely accepted before, during and after the experiments. Telepathy is usually defined today as 'the acquisition (through nonsensory means) by a person of information that could only originate *in the mind* of another'. While earlier definitions of the term might not have been as precisely formulated, they conformed to the 'spirit' of this definition. That there were nonphysical entities, called minds or souls, and that there was direct interaction between them, provided the working hypothesis that led to the experiments; and it is only appropriate that they be seen as either confirming or disconfirming the hypothesis.

There is hardly any doubt that the 'founding fathers' of psychical research intended their work to establish that the universe had a nonphysical dimension; and the attempted demonstration of telepathy as a fact should be seen as a means to that end. Quite apart from this historical perspective, however, the vast majority of those working in this field take the view—rightly or wrongly—that ESP phenomena in general, and telepathy in particular, if established as genuine, will prove that man and nature have a nonphysical component. Take, for example, the well-known assertion by Price that 'there is no room for telepathy in a materialistic universe'.[3] Similarly, Rhine says,[4] ' . . . the experimental results of these psi studies present phenomena from human life that *require* the rejection of the conception of man as a wholly physical system' : and again, in a later work,[5] he speaks of the 'refutation of the philosophy of materialism' that parapsychology has achieved.

At the same time one also finds various suggestions to the effect that ESP ability (and hence telepathy) in man may be of evolutionary origin. Rhine, for one, has come out with this suggestion in many of his works. For example, in his *New World of the Mind*,[6] he says :

'The results (of ESP experiments) just reviewed seem to indicate afresh, that here is being dealt with something not localised, not recently acquired, not a surface feature, but something very basic, something springing from far down the stem of psychological origins . . . Psi seems to involve a submerged order of activity overlaid by the later developments of evolutionary progress'.

Again, engaging in 'some useful exploratory generalisation regarding *psi* and the science of life' in a recent work,[7] he says, 'For example one immediately suspects that the point of origin of *psi* must have been far back in evolutionary history, long before man himself arrived.'

Another notable scientist who has consistently made this suggestion over a long period is Sir Alister Hardy. He seems to have held, since at least 1949, that if telepathy were established as a natural power or ability of animals, it would help us understand better the whole process of evolution, particularly what is known as 'organic selection'. This process—whereby a segment of an animal population acquires new organs, thus sometimes giving rise to a new species—presupposes 'behavioural selection', that is the process by which an animal population acquires new habits or modes of behaviour. The selection of habits, while it is partly, even largely, brought about by the new environmental conditions in which the population finds itself, must, according to Hardy, have an 'internal' cause as well. This is provided by the inquisitive exploratory nature of animals. Whichever way the new habits are formed, only when they have become fully instinctive can they be controlled and passed on by the genetic constitution of the animals. But 'the mechanism whereby new habits do spread through populations' initially, needs to be fully understood. Imitation is, of course, an important part of this mechanism, but, additionally, something like telepathy seems to be strongly suggested, if not required, as a component. As he says :[8]

'Actually there can be little doubt that truly instinctive behaviour is governed by the DNA gene complex, probably built in by organic selection from gradually formed habits of increasing elaboration. These habits, however, before being genetically fixed, might be spread and stabilised in the population by some such telepathy-like means, for we have seen that they must become widespread before they can be so incorporated'.

The question that particularly interests me and the one that I intend to explore here is this. If telepathy is of evolutionary origin, can it at the same time be an ability exercised by *minds*, as has been claimed to be the case? If not, why not? If yes, what sort of theory of mind do we require in order to 'accommodate' the implications of the evolutionary origin of telepathy?

II

Before embarking on my main task, however, it may be appropriate to see what grounds there may be for supporting the claim that telepathy is of evolutionary origin. I have already referred to Hardy's reasons for suggesting that telepathy may have a function in the whole process of evolution. There is, besides, a sizeable and growing literature on what has come to be known as 'anpsi', i.e. the investigation of the so-called psychic powers of animals. Elsewhere in this volume[9] some of these experiments have been discussed. I will, therefore, briefly refer only to those phenomena which ostensibly provide evidence for telepathy as such in animals. But before I do so, perhaps I should add that even those experiments in 'anpsi' that are not specifically designed to test telepathic ability may, if successful, increase the *a priori* probability of animals having this ability. For if it is established that animals have ESP ability of some sort, then since telepathy is an ESP ability, it will be more probable that they have the latter. In any case, there are phenomena which, it is claimed, indicate telepathic ability in animals. To start with, there is the well-known conviction among animal lovers, particularly owners of pets, that animals—usually dogs and cats—often behave in ways which can only be seen as response to the unexpressed thoughts and feelings of their masters at a particular time. The sudden change of direction of a flock of birds in flight was suspected by Edmund Selous[10] to be brought about by telepathic 'communication' among the birds. The dog, Chris, investigated by Dr Pratt is claimed to have displayed impressive telepathic ability;[11] similarly the horse, Lady, investigated by the Rhines.[12] Bechterev's telepathy experiments with dogs[13] and perhaps Osis' experiments with cats[14] seem to point in the same direction. I do not intend to assess the results of these experiments here. But I do feel constrained to point out that in most of them the results could well be, wholly or partly, attributed to the animals' ability to respond to the involuntary muscular and other 'cues' emanating from the humans involved in the experiments. This possibility has in fact been acknowledged by some of the experimenters themselves.

At any rate the phenomena cited so far claim to show telepathic ability only in animals. The experiments of Cleve Backster,[15] on the other hand, indicate the possession of telepathic powers by plants as well, and indeed by every living cell. These experiments are interesting and challenging, and since they have not been discussed in the rest of this volume, I shall briefly describe them here without going into the minutiae of the experimental set-up. The first indication of the possession of ESP ability by plants came, according to Backster, quite by accident. Out of simple curiosity, he once decided 'to measure the rate at which water rose in a plant from the root area into the leaf', by the use of a polygraph. This machine is used to record through a tracing on a graph a person's 'psychogalvanic reflex' (PGR) or the 'galvanic skin response' (GSR) in certain behavioural situations; and is used to administer the so-called 'lie-detector test'. Since Backster's professional work related to polygraphs, the machine was readily available. He secured an electrode on each side of a leaf of a *dracaena massangeana* plant so that the leaf was sandwiched between the electrodes. 'Contrary to the author's expectation, from the outset the plant leaf tracing exhibited a downward trend. Then, after approximately one minute of chart-time, the tracing exhibited a contour similar to a reaction pattern typical of a human subject experiencing an emotional stimulation of a short duration.' Backster figured that if this finding actually indicated an 'emotional' response on the part of the plant, then he should perhaps expose the plant to something similar to the 'threat-to-well-being' principle in order to get a more definitive result. This he did by first immersing another leaf into a cup of hot coffee. Nothing very noticeable happened. After a while he decided to obtain a match actually to burn the plant leaf being tested; and 'at the instant of this decision . . . there was a dramatic change in the tracing pattern in the form of an abrupt and prolonged upward sweep of the recording pen'. Since at that time Backster was not in contact either with the plant or the machine, apparently the plant was 'responding telepathically' to the thought of the harm he intended to inflict on it. Similar results were obtained in later experiments.

Through more complex, (more or less) completely automated experiments, Backster seemed also to get confirmation for his hypothesis that plants responded to imminent harm to other organisms in the vicinity. With the use of several machines simultaneously, he tested the reactions of three different plants to the forthcoming killing, by immersion in hot water, of several shrimps. Since in these experiments the times of extermination were determined by a randomiser and the killing itself performed mechanically, it would seem that the plants' 'knowledge' of the impending harm to the shrimps must have been derived through either clairvoyance or precognition. The results of these experiments are best summed up in Backster's own words.

'Based upon Backster Research Foundation observations during a period of approximately three years, and on research currently in progress, the author hypothesises that this perception facility may be part of a primary sensory system capable of functioning at cell level. This is further suggested by observation of its apparent presence in plant and animal tissue separated from an organism (including human), and maintained *in vitro* where the specialised senses are not present.'

It seems that, if Backster's experiments have produced genuine effects, plants are endowed with telepathic, and possibly other forms of ESP, ability.

Unless alternative explanations of all the above-mentioned data are found to be entirely satisfactory, it would seem that there are grounds for believing that such diverse species in the animal kingdom as man, mice, cats, dogs, horses, birds, jirds, ants, bees and cockroaches all have some degree of psi, including telepathic ability. Indeed if we accept Backster's findings, then plants are no exception. This widespread distribution would tend to make a formidable case for the claim that telepathy is of evolutionary origin. For if we are not to take this distribution simply as a staggering coincidence—a methodologically infertile supposition—we have to explain it by tracing telepathy back to some common progenitor from which it has been inherited, perhaps as an instrument of survival. Such reasoning is well established in evolutionary theory, and there would seem to be no good reason to make an exception in this case.

III

It is only fair to say that the evidence so far is neither in quantity nor quality adequate to establish the evolutionary account of telepathy as a scientific fact. But suppose it were? At least two conclusions would seem to be inescapable :

(*a*) Telepathy must, *in principle*, be a *universal* ability inherited by *all* forms of organic life. This conclusion becomes hard to avoid, especially in view of the fact that (à la Backster) even plants, the earliest forms of life, seem to have it; and if plants have it, then it would be inconsistent not to hold that all animal species, however primitive in the evolutionary scale, have it too. Negatively, it would seem to follow that an explanation of the 'mechanics' of telepathy in terms of any property, faculty or process which is (either by definition, common consent or on the authority of science) deemed to be exclusive to a single species of animals, say man, is bound to be wrong.

(b) Telepathy must also, *in principle*, be a *normal* or natural ability of all forms of life, which one would expect organisms to use (and display) in coping with all the situations it was 'designed' —in its evolutionary history—to cope with. It can hardly be transmitted by the gene complex without first being fully established as instinctive; and what is truly instinctive has to be recognised as a natural or normal ability or propensity of animals. As with other instincts, there should be no 'mystery' about why they have it, but rather why they do not show it on occasions which otherwise seem to require the use of this ability or faculty. We know nothing about why and for what situations it might have been 'designed'. But to speculate, since it evidently seems to go back to a stage which is prior to the full growth of the sensori-motor complex, it would be plausible to expect this ability to come into play whenever a situation is so daunting or novel that the sensori-motor complex cannot deal with it efficiently; or when this complex has been badly impaired or is threatened with imminent impairment; or perhaps when the use of this complex has, by some specially acquired skill, been put 'in abeyance'.

If my argument so far is correct, then it would seem that the theory of the evolutionary origin of telepathy will, in some sense, require (a) and (b) as basic principles. In the rest of this paper I shall refer to (a) as the *Universality Principle,* and (b) as the *Normality Principle*. We are now in a position to work out the implications of these principles for a theory of mind that could be said to explain telepathy adequately. We shall start with the Universality Principle.

It seems evident that we now have a set of mutually inconsistent propositions :

(1) Telepathy is an ability exercised by minds (if current definitions of telepathy are to be accepted).

(II) Only human beings are endowed with minds (this seems to be true by 'common consent', if not by definition).

(III) Telepathy is a universal ability possessed by all organisms, and not just human beings (Universality Principle).

Assuming that those who suggest an evolutionary origin of telepathy are right, and also that my earlier argument is valid, we cannot challenge the truth of (III). For the purposes of this paper, then, I shall take (III) to be true. That means that either (I) or (II) must be false.

To the extent that the word 'mind' is regarded as synonymous, and hence interchangeable, with 'soul' or 'psyche', a number of scientists and philosophers will be in favour of rejecting (I) as false. They will insist that we either eliminate the word 'mind' from our vocabulary; or else, if we must keep it, take it to refer—euphemistically, if you like—to the brain or brain-processes. For, they will argue, there are no such things as nonphysical minds, souls or psyches. And possibly they are right. In that case we have to conclude that telepathy is not, strictly speaking, a function of minds or psyches. Consequently, any definition of telepathy which makes it an operation of minds can no longer be correct, unless, of course, 'mind' is simply a convenient referring expression for 'brain-processes'.

This indeed would be the view of some materialists and of those who espouse 'physical radiation' models for ESP. It is not my intention to discuss here the case for or against materialism. So I will simply point out two reasons which, for the purposes of this paper, will allow me to disregard the materialist alternative. Firstly, it has been argued reasonably convincingly that a physical radiation model of ESP is implausible,[16] if not absurd. Secondly, in view of the anti-materialist assumptions of the pioneers of psychical research as well as of the majority of psychical researchers today, the materialist alternative would be, to say the least, a drastic step and such a drastic step cannot be said to be forced on us as long as there is yet another alternative to be considered.

That brings us to the last of the alternatives, namely the rejection of (II) and, by implication, the acceptance of the proposition that all living beings have minds, souls or psyches. Is there any reason why animals, plants—indeed all forms of life—cannot be said to have minds? Popular opinion in the West might indeed resist this idea, and even find it utterly repugnant, since this would tend to put animals and plants 'on a par' with human beings in a very important way. That would be detrimental to the Judaeo-Christian conviction that man was created to be unique and clearly superior to the rest of creatures in the universe. But there seem to be no good grounds for hoping that this belief will survive the test of time any more successfully than the traditional notion that the earth was the centre of the universe (and hence the sun must revolve round it); or the belief that Darwinism must be false because it impugned the idea of special creation. Most of the Indian religions—Hinduism, Buddhism[17] Jainism—include the possession of a soul by every living creature among their basic tenets of belief. Even in the West, vitalists like Henry Bergson, Hans Driesch and, to some extent, Aristotle have entertained similar views. The idea, then, that every organism has a mind or psyche is not absurd[18] or unheard of; and it would seem unreasonable to reject it on purely sentimental grounds.

It seems then that the Universality Principle entails that if there is a nonphysical reality in nature which makes telepathy possible, it cannot be considered an exclusive privilege of *homo sapiens*. Any traditional dualist or immaterialist system could, it seems, satisfy this principle, provided it conceded that all living beings have minds. Even traditional Cartesianism would only need to be revised rather than rejected. But the implications of the Normality Principle would, I suspect, be almost impossible to accommodate within the framework of Cartesianism.

One of the fundamentals of Cartesianism is the belief that every mind is unique and distinct from every other. It thinks its own thoughts, enjoys or suffers its own experiences, and interacts only with its own body. It can acquire some knowledge of other bodies (at least, it can hope to) through its senses, but direct (non-inferential) knowledge of other minds is not just abnormal or exceptional but *impossible*. The doctrine of 'privileged access' has been rightly regarded as an inevitable consequence of Cartesianism. The Normality Principle which stipulates that communication between minds is in principle absolutely normal and natural, is evidently incompatible with Cartesianism. If this 'private access' doctrine were simply a consequence of Cartesianism, then by rejecting the latter one would have disposed of the former. But unfortunately, this easy way out seems to be blocked. Whatever its origins, the doctrine is now firmly implanted as essential to the way we think about minds and mental operations; it can be said to be embedded in our conceptual framework. Any account of telepathy, therefore, must, it seems to me, make some concession to this doctrine. It will appear then that since a mind can only witness (directly) its own thoughts, *for telepathy to occur the two ostensibly different minds in 'communication', must, in some important sense, be one.* Likewise, if all organisms are in principle able to 'communicate' telepathically—any one of them with any other—then it would seem that their apparently many minds must somehow be one. Paradoxical as it may seem, telepathy demands, on the one hand, that there be distinct minds, for otherwise all occurrences of so-called telepathy will only be cases of introspection or self-analysis. On the other hand, it demands that these distinct minds be only *apparently* distinct, for otherwise they cannot communicate or interact; and telepathy can then never be normal or even possible. It will remain a puzzling phenomenon, an exception to the rule or principle, a mystery to be 'swallowed' as such but not understood.

IV

If we now put together the respective requirements of the Universality Principle and the Normality Principle, we should have to accept not only that every organism has a mind, but, additionally, that all these ostensibly distinct minds are essentially one and the same. I have already indicated that Cartesianism is unlikely to meet these requirements. Indeed, as far as I can see, there is hardly any traditional or current philosophy of mind which incorporates these features. But let us briefly look at some likely 'candidates'.

Mundle has suggested[19] that Berkeley's form of idealism seems better equipped than Cartesianism to explain ESP. Can this idealism offer a philosophy of mind with the features that we are looking for? I have grave doubts that it can. It would seem very dubious to suggest that Berkeley, a bishop, would have favoured or tolerated the attribution of minds or souls to creatures other than man. It would certainly have been outrageous to him to con-template that all these minds, including those of plants, were essentially one with the infinite mind of God. There is a sense in which Berkeley's philosophy renders telepathy normal : in a world where every transaction occurs according to regularities which can be changed by the will of God, it does not make sense to ask why telepathy occurs any more than why it does not. But to invoke God to explain problems in parapsychology is to give up any intention on its part to become and remain a science; and I do not believe that parapsychologists have given up yet. Spinoza's pyscho-physical parallelism is not a theory I can honestly claim to understand too well. But I strongly suspect that it falls between the two stools of materialism (particularly its 'identity theory' version) and theistic dualism (in which God establishes the harmony between matter and mind and between mind and mind). To the extent that it is neither, it is hardly an explanatory theory.[20]

The doctrine of emergence could satisfy the Universality Principle if it allowed that the emergence of life was parallel to and/or linked with that of mind. But I cannot see this doctrine being able to accommodate the requirement of one mind. If there is just one mind, 'bits' of which, as it were, 'attach' themselves to every single organism as it evolves, then surely the mind is a 'pre-existent' rather than an 'emergent' entity. The doctrine of the 'Collective Unconscious' may seem to answer our need here, for while it allows distinct minds, it also requires a 'common mind' (the collective or 'racial' unconscious). But I believe that the doctrine is question-begging in character : it does not explain how the Collective Un-conscious becomes possible in the first place. Does it require the operation of telepathy ?

There is one philosophical system, however, from which a judicious selection of certain features could go some way towards meeting the requirements of the case. I am referring to the *Advaita Vedanta* of Shamkara, the eighth-century Indian philosopher. He speaks of all individual souls (*atman*) as being literally part of one universal soul (*Brahman*). Every living creature has an *atman*, but the *atman* without a body will not be an individual. Indeed when an *atman* becomes completely disembodied, i.e. it has neither a gross nor a subtle body, it then becomes 'liberated' and merges into the universal soul. This world-soul, or *Brahman*, is eternal and uncreated, but impersonal. Personality, like individuality, presupposes embodiment. Such an impersonal principle cannot act, will, or desire. It simply *is* and has consciousness and 'bliss'. Whatever the cause of the 'splitting' of this universal soul into many individual souls,[21] one consequence of this is embodiment for the latter. Bits of the universal soul become 'trapped', as it were, by the various bodies, and thus separate into distinct units. But they are all parts of the same soul or 'mind-stuff'.[22] It is clear that this system has both the features required by our two principles : every organism has a soul; and the souls of all organisms, while 'encapsulated' in different bodies, are essentially parts of one and the same' soul-substance'.

On this sort of account it is more appropriate to ask why telepathy does not actually occur all the time; and the answer would seem to lie in the fact of embodiment. Bodies, it would seem, not only divide the one soul into many, but even 'insulate' one individual soul from another. It is important to note, however, that this separation of souls and their consequent insularity, while mostly effective, is not final. If it were final, then, of course the merging of these souls with the universal soul, i.e. their liberation, would be impossible. And that, according to Shamkara, is clearly not the case. Individual souls do attain liberation, sometimes even while they are embodied. Knowledge by the *atman* of its essential unity with *Brahman*, it seems, renders the body impotent in the exercise of its insulating function. The 'breaking of the barriers' imposed by the body becomes final in the state of liberation. But the voluntary 'weakening' of this barrier for short periods can evidently be achieved by the practice of Yoga. This is what the Indian Yogic tradition would have us believe. Perhaps the states of deep dreamless sleep, involuntary trance, hypnosis, even dreaming, and telepathy are, in different ways, instances of the 'failure of the insulating function' of the bodies in question.

It is very risky to construct a physical model of what is supposedly a nonphysical entity. But in the hope that this fact will not be lost sight of, I will suggest a partial model. It is as though the soul were, like air, one continuous substance 'extending' through the universe, parts of which become trapped inside enclosures (bodies) which *normally* do not let the outside air in or the inside air out. Consequently 'perturbations' occurring in one part of this substance which should in principle have reached every other part, do not normally succeed in doing so because of the 'insulating' function of the bodies. But under certain circumstances the insulating mechanism fails, wholly or partly. These, it would seem, are the occasions when telepathy actually occurs. It is well known that the efficient generation and distribution of electricity, as we know it today, was brought about largely by better knowledge of insulating materials and of the principles and techniques of insulation. Could this have a bearing on the future work of psychical researchers, especially of those preoccupied with telepathy?

V

What are my conclusions, then? It should be evident that they can only be stated hypothetically. If telepathy is of evolutionary origin, and if it involves the operation of nonphysical minds or psyches, then, I have argued, we require a philosophical theory which, in relevant respects, resembles that of Shamkara.[23] An evolutionary account of telepathy can be reconciled with some form of dualism; and I have tried to work out the 'price' that, it seems to me, must be paid for such a reconciliation. I confess that to many the 'price' may seem too high, and they may be tempted to regard my conclusions as a *reductio ad absurdum* disproof of either the evolutionary account of telepathy, or of dualism, or indeed of the whole notion of telepathy. I think they will be perfectly free to do so provided they can justify the need to do so on rational, not emotive, grounds.

Assuming that the dualism outlined above can survive legitimate criticism, it would have been interesting to explore whether it has any advantages over its rivals in explaining other 'paranormal' phenomena like clairvoyance, precognition and psychokinesis. I cannot now see that it has any obvious disadvantages. But detailed exploration of this will be a major exercise which I cannot hope to accomplish in the space at my disposal now. So I shall end by saying that, with or without dualism, the Normality Principle perhaps deserves to be made a methodological assumption by psychical researchers. In respect of telepathy, this assumption would consist in regarding telepathy as, in principle, normal (as against 'paranormal'), and then asking what stops it. Such a reversal of perspective on methodological grounds has in the past often proved extremely fruitful. Modern science owes not a little to Galileo assuming perpetual motion in bodies and then asking what makes them stop. If he had persisted with the old Aristotelian search for the cause of every single motion, there would have been no concept of inertia, friction, gravitation and a host of others. Perhaps parapsychology needs to adopt this procedure self-consciously, and in hope. Rhine speaks[24] of psi phenomena representing a 'Copernican order of revolution'. Will my suggestion about telepathy, then, represent a revolution within a revolution?

REFERENCES AND NOTES

(1) G. J. Warnock (ed.), *The Philosophy of Perception* (London, 1967), p. 2.
(2) A. G. N. Flew, *A New Approach to Psychical Research* (London, 1953), p. 118.
(3) H. H. Price, 'Psychical Research and Human Personality', *The Hibbert Journal*, vol. 47 (1949), p. 109.
(4) J. B. Rhine, 'On Parapsychology and the Nature of Man', in *Dimensions of Mind*, Sidney Hook (ed.), (London, 1969), p. 77.
(5) J. B. Rhine, 'Parapsychology and Man', *The Journal of Parapsychology*, vol. 36 (1972), p. 116.
(6) J. B. Rhine, *New World of the Mind* (London, 1954), p. 111
(7) J. B. Rhine, 'Parapsychology and Man', op. cit., p. 109.
(8) Alister Hardy, 'Biology and ESP', in *Science and ESP,* J. R. Smythies (ed.), (London, 1967), p. 157.
(9) See the contributions by Gauld and Mundle in this volume.
(10) Edmund Selous, *Thought Transference, or What, in Birds?* (London, 1931).
(11) J. G. Pratt, *Parapsychology: An Insider's View of ESP* (New York, 1964).
(12) J. B. Rhine and L. E. Rhine, 'An investigation of a "mindreading" horse', *Journal of Abnormal Social Psychology,* 23 (1929), pp. 449–66, and 24 (1929), pp. 287–92.
(13) W. Bechterev, ' "Direct influence" of a person upon the behaviour of animals', *Journal of Parapsychology*, vol. 13 (1949), pp. 166–76.
(14) K. Osis, 'A test of the occurrence of a psi effect between man and the cat', *Journal of Parapsychology,* vol. 16 (1952), pp. 223–56.
(15) Cleve Backster, 'Evidence Of A Primary Perception In Plant Life', *International Journal of Parapsychology*, vol. X (1968), pp. 329–48.
(16) See, for instance, C. D. Broad, *Religion, Philosophy and Psychical Research* (London, 1953), pp. 38–9; also, Gauld, in this volume, pp. 30–31.
(17) This is, of course, not true of those schools of Buddhism which subscribe to *anatmavada,* the doctrine that there is no soul.

(18) It is possible to take the view, as some do, that the very idea of a soul or psyche is absurd or incoherent. If this view is correct, then naturally the claim that every organism has a soul is absurd too.

(19) C. W. K. Mundle, 'The Explanation of ESP', in *Science and ESP* op. cit., pp. 205–6.

(20) I am basically in agreement with the view of Abraham Edel, 'Theory-Categories in the Mind-Body Problem', in *Dimension of Mind*, op. cit., p. 95.

(21) According to Shamkara the separation of *atman from Brahman* is caused by *Avidya*, or ignorance, which results in embodiment for the soul.

(22) In an important sense, it is quite inappropriate to speak of 'mind-stuff' in the context of Shamkara. For in his system, as in most of the orthodox Indian philosophical systems, the mind (*manas*) is taken to be quite distinct from the soul (*atman*), the former being clearly physical. So one should really be talking of 'soul-stuff', if anything. But in view of the fact that in the Western philosophical tradition the mind is not distinguished from the soul, I have chosen to use the more familiar term 'mind-stuff'.

(23) Since Shamkara was an idealist who did not accept the ultimate reality of any form of matter, it is evident that in retaining real material bodies, and hence a physical nature, coexistent with the universal soul or mind-stuff—as indeed in so many other respects—I have departed considerably from his system of philosophy. But then there is no reason why one should go with him all the way in the present context.

(24) J. B. Rhine, 'Parapsychology', in *The New Outline of Modern Knowlege*, Alan Pryce-Jones (ed.), (London, 1956), p. 205.

INDEX